THE

ULTIMATE

HOLLYWOOD

TOUR BOOK

THE ULTIMATE

HOLLYWOOD

TOUR BOOK

**THE INCOMPARABLE GUIDE TO
MOVIE STARS' HOMES,
MOVIE AND TV LOCATIONS,
SCANDALS, MURDERS,
SUICIDES, AND ALL
THE FAMOUS TOURIST SITES**

WILLIAM A. GORDON

NORTH RIDGE BOOKS
El Toro, CA

OTHER BOOKS BY WILLIAM A. GORDON

SHOT ON THIS SITE
A Traveler's Guide to the Places and Locations Used to
Film Famous Movies and Television Shows

THE FOURTH OF MAY
Killings and Coverups at Kent State
(hardcover edition)

FOUR DEAD IN OHIO
Was There a Conspiracy at Kent State?
(paperback reprint)

"HOW MANY BOOKS DO YOU SELL IN OHIO?"
A Quote Book for Writers

In Memory of
Professor Dennis Gordon
1915-1989

Tour groups interested in special sales, promotions, or in creating customized tours may contact us at the above address or e-mail us at NRBooks@aol.com.

Second Edition 1997
10

Library of Congress Cataloging-in-Publication Data
  Gordon, William A.
  The ultimate Hollywood tour book: the incomparable guide to
  movie stars' homes, movie and TV locations, scandals, murders,
  suicides, and all the famous tourist sites / William A. Gordon—
  Second Ed.
  p.cm.
  ISBN 0-937813-06-0
    1.   Motion picture actors and actresses—Homes and haunts—
California—Los Angeles—Guidebooks. 2. Motion picture
locations—California—Los Angeles—Guidebooks. 3. Hollywood
(Los Angeles, Calif.)—Guidebooks. 4. Motion picture actors and
actresses—Biography—Miscellanea. 5. Hollywood (Los Angeles,
Calif.)-Social life and customs.
I. Title
PN 1993.5.U65G635 1992
791.43'09794'940904 9—dc20

ISBN 0-937813-06-0
LC 97-65351

CONTENTS

INTRODUCTION 9
BEVERLY HILLS, BEL-AIR AND
    HOLMBY HILLS 16
BRENTWOOD 67
PACIFIC PALISADES 75
MALIBU 82
SANTA MONICA AND VENICE 96
CULVER CITY 105
WESTWOOD AND CENTURY CITY 107
THE SUNSET STRIP 118
WEST HOLLYWOOD 133
HOLLYWOOD 142
FAIRFAX AND THE MIRACLE MILE 167
HANCOCK PARK AND
    THE WILSHIRE DISTRICT.......................171
MULHOLLAND DRIVE AND
    THE HOLLYWOOD HILLS........................178
HOLLYWOODLAND AND LOS FELIZ 188
DOWNTOWN 198
PASADENA 210
BURBANK AND TOLUCA LAKE 221
UNIVERSAL CITY, NORTH HOLLYWOOD
    AND STUDIO CITY 229
SHERMAN OAKS, VAN NUYS AND ENCINO....233
OTHER POINTS OF INTEREST
    IN OR NEAR LOS ANGELES 239
ACKNOWLEDGMENTS 247
INDEX...255

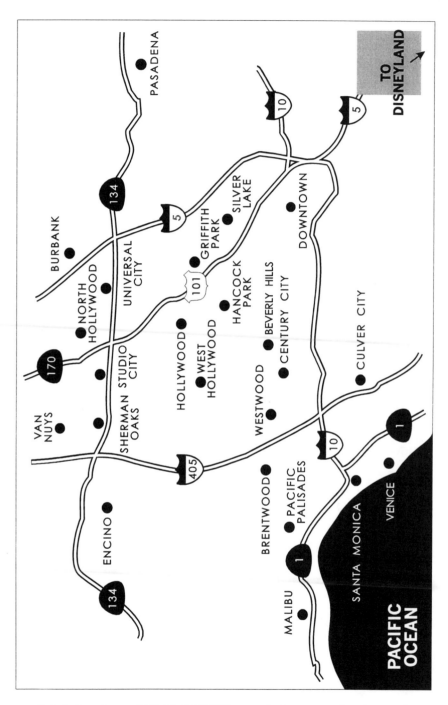

MAP 1 GREATER LOS ANGELES

INTRODUCTION

The Ultimate Hollywood Tour Book was written for the millions of people who visit Southern California each year, and who, not knowing how to find the real attractions of Tinseltown, take prepackaged bus tours to celebrities' homes or who go on studio tours which show you only what the studios want you to see.

This book will take you to places you will not be shown on any organized tour. We will show you where the major stars of both today and yesteryear live (or have lived). Stars such as Madonna, Elvis Presley, Marilyn Monroe, Arnold Schwarzenegger, and Tom Cruise.

The Ultimate Hollywood Tour Book will show you where you have the best chances of actually seeing the stars. Although it is always fun to see where they live, you probably will not see them outside their gated mansions and homes. However, there is a good chance you will see someone famous if you go to one of the restaurants, hotels or hot spots that attract a celebrity clientele. Dozens of such establishments are profiled in this book.

We will show you where, throughout greater Los Angeles, dozens of classic or highly popular motion pictures have been filmed. Movies such as *E.T., Pretty Woman, Independence Day, Speed, The Nutty Professor, Volcano, Die Hard, The Terminator, Terminator II, In the Line of Fire,* the *Back to the Future* series, the *Beverly Hills Cop* series, *Chinatown,* and *Father of the Bride.*

We will show you how to find famous locations such as the "L.A. Law Building," "The Bat Cave," and the houses or apartments seen in popular television shows: "Melrose Place," "Dynasty," "The Brady Bunch," "Seinfeld," and "Beverly Hills 90210."

We will show you where some of Hollywood's most notorious murders, suicides and scandals have occurred. You will see where O. J. Simpson allegedly murdered his ex-wife Nicole and her friend Ron Goldman; where the Manson clan struck (in a home Candice Bergen lived in just a few months earlier); where Marilyn Monroe, John Belushi, Janis Joplin, and River Phoenix fatally overdosed; and where the Menendez brothers gunned down their parents in cold blood.

We will take you to other locations that may surprise you. How many of you know, for example, that John Dean, the man who brought down Richard Nixon's presidency, now lives in Beverly Hills? Or that Nixon himself lived in Brentwood after losing the 1960 election? Would you like to see where John F. Kennedy's most notorious mistress lived? Or where Ronald Reagan lived when he was elected president—or his retirement home? Virtually all of Reagan's Hollywood residences can be found in this book.

We will also show you how to find the major studios and world-famous attractions such as Mann's Chinese Theaters and the popular Universal Studios tour.

The focus of this book, of course, is not on the commercial attractions or the usual tourist traps. The tours and the television ticket outlets are included because you cannot write a guide book about Hollywood and not mention them.

The emphasis in this book is on the hidden or unpublicized attractions—the ones that Hollywood insiders know about, but which tourists usually never know exist.

An important point needs to be made at the outset. When I refer to Hollywood, both in the title and throughout the book, I refer not just to the geographical community within the city of Los Angeles where most of early motion picture history was made. I refer to Hollywood, the entertainment industry, which today is spread out throughout all of Southern California.

Ironically, many tourists find Hollywood, the community, to be the most disappointing part of their trips. Many tourists come to Hollywood looking for movie stars, glamorous settings and palm trees. What they often find instead are tacky souvenir shops and teen-agers who look like they have taken too many drugs.

I certainly do not want to suggest that little of note happens in Hollywood the community today, that Hollywood is not making good progress revitalizing itself, or that the community is not worth seeing. In fact, I cannot imagine anyone touring Southern California and not seeing Hollywood the community.

The point here is simply that this book focuses on the present. And while I have tried to pay homage to Hollywood's past (particularly its glamour days in the 1920s, 1930s and 1940s), this is primarily a book on how today's Hollywood lives, works and plays.

This book is arranged geographically, and starts with a self-guided tour of the celebrity homes in the so-called Platinum Triangle: Beverly Hills, Bel-Air and the lesser known, but actually more expensive residential area, Holmby Hills.

Maps to these celebrity homes are hawked on seemingly every street corner along Sunset Boulevard and in every souvenir shop in town. The tour presented in this book is very different than what those maps offer. For one, the maps in this book are up to date (and are updated in each edition). More importantly, the addresses have been verified through searches of public records.

The Ultimate Hollywood Tour Book is also the first Hollywood tour book to show not only where the major celebrities of the past and present live (or have lived), but also to tell something about the history of these homes.

(Incidentally, the people who sell the maps to the stars' homes would have you believe that most motion picture and television stars live in Beverly Hills or Bel-Air. Actually, only about 25% of the best-known living actors live on the streets covered in the "Maps to the Stars' Homes." As this book shows, celebrities live all over greater Los Angeles. Observant readers will also note that the younger stars tend to live in the Hollywood Hills and in the outlying areas. Hardly any celebrity under the age of 40 lives in Beverly Hills.)

Subsequent chapters highlight celebrity homes, movie locations, historic entertainment industry sites, and other points of interest in Brentwood, Pacific Palisades, Malibu, Venice and Santa Monica, Culver City, Westwood and Century City, the Sunset Strip and West Hollywood, Fairfax and the Miracle Mile, Hancock Park and the Wilshire District, downtown Los Angeles, the Hollywood Hills, Pasadena, the San Fernando Valley, and, of course, Hollywood itself.

Although the tours presented here very roughly circle the city, the author realizes that tourists will start from many different points of town and will, instead of following any sequence presented, tour the areas that are either closest to them or are of most interest to them.

To make the most of your trip to Los Angeles, I suggest reading this book first, choosing the areas of greatest interest, and using the maps provided, combining the tours as you see fit. (For example, tours of the Sunset Strip and Beverly Hills tours can be very easily combined.)

There is really a great deal to see—and you will find, despite rumors to the contrary, that Los Angeles is one of the greatest places in the world to go sightseeing.

In fact, that is why I live here: because I get to go sightseeing every day.

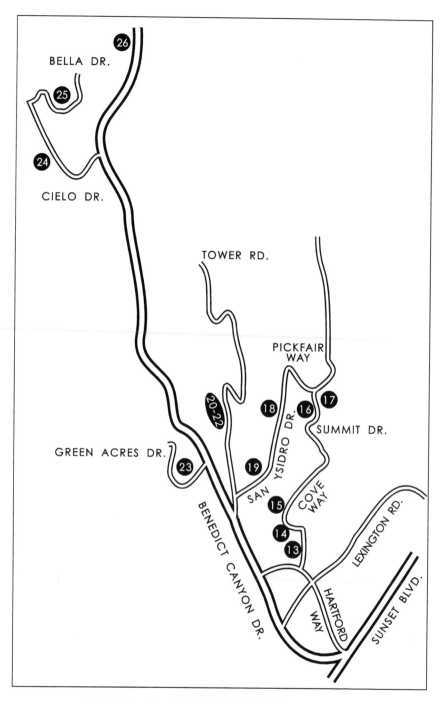

MAP 3   BEVERLY HILLS

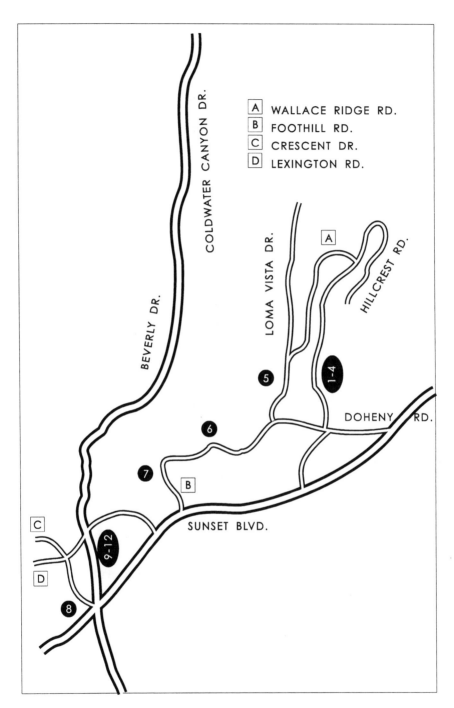

MAP 2 BEVERLY HILLS

BEVERLY HILLS, BEL-AIR AND HOLMBY HILLS

Whenever I show people around Beverly Hills, I like to get behind certain tour buses, tell my passengers what the tour guides are saying, and then let my passengers know who really lives in these homes.

I do not mean to suggest that most of the tours are unreliable, or in any way disreputable (although I have heard one person indirectly affiliated with one major tour joke about "the new lies our guides are making up this week").

I am merely suggesting that the tour guides—usually aspiring actors between gigs—have, on occasion, used their highly creative talents when telling people about who lives where in Beverly Hills.

Tour guides have been known to move celebrities from one street to another—or from one part of town to another—just to spice up the tours. One might say that they sometimes play a version of celebrity musical chairs just to have something to say while driving on streets where no one particularly notable has lived on.

Of course, there is another, probably even more important reason why the tours of Beverly Hills do not always meet the highest standards of accuracy. That is because the tours are based on the maps to the stars' homes. The maps—which have been around since at least 1924 (real estate agents used to publish them themselves to lure prospective homebuyers to Beverly Hills)—are an inescapable part of life in L.A. They are hawked on seemingly every street corner along Sunset Boulevard in Beverly Hills and in virtually every souvenir shop along Hollywood Boulevard. You can even find the maps in vending machines at the public information center of the Los Angeles Convention and Visitors Bureau.

The best-selling map is called simply "Map of Movie Stars' Homes." Even though celebrities move as often, if not more often, than regular folk, the current edition is remarkably similar to a 1977 edition of the same map on file at the Beverly Hills Public Library.

The reason the mapmakers do not keep up with celebrity comings and goings is because they have no incentive to. After all, their customers never know the difference. Tourists who are in town for a short period do not have the time nor the inclination to independently verify the information they are given—even if they knew how to.

Of course, there are a few people in Hollywood who like to keep up with the latest celebrity real estate transactions. You are lucky. I happen to be one of them.

The following tour, which tourists can follow in lieu of paying $20 to $30 to go on a bus tour, brings Beverly Hills touring up to date and reflects who lives, or has lived, in the houses in Beverly Hills, Bel-Air and Holmby Hills, each time we go back to press (which is at least once a year).

I have included driving directions to help the reader get around Beverly Hills, but I have not do so for most other parts of town. Beverly Hills is a special case. Its residential streets twist and turn so much that they often look like pretzels. Not only are the streets sometimes confusing for the uninitiated, but several of the streets change names in midcourse—and sometimes more than once.

A recent story in the *Los Angeles Times* told the story of typical tourists who found following the existing maps to stars' homes so frustrating that they gave up and went to the beach instead.

The directions which accompany the text and maps should make your sightseeing a more enjoyable experience.

Please note: These houses are private residences. You can drive by them, admire them, and be what we call a "lookie-loo;" but you should never, ever disturb the privacy of these individuals.

If you approach a celebrity at his or her home, he or she may construe the approach as a hostile act and act accordingly.

Remember: not all celebrities are as volatile as Sean Penn or Sean Young. But why take a chance?

Also: while it is always possible you may see celebrities outside their houses (I've seen Madonna jogging, Ted Danson's kids playing, and Valerie Harper walking her dogs), any such sightings are strictly up to chance. The likelihood is that you will not see celebrities outside their homes.

If you want to see movie stars, go to one of the many restaurants or hotels they frequent. This book lists dozens of establishments where you have a good chance of seeing someone famous.

The following tour should be taken just to get a general sense of how and where celebrities and Los Angeles' upper class live.

(DIRECTIONS: This tour starts at the intersection of Sunset Boulevard and Hillcrest Drive, which is located one mile east of Beverly Hills Hotel and just west of the Sunset Strip. You will be traveling north on Hillcrest Drive. If you are on Sunset headed east, make a left turn onto Hillcrest Drive. If you are coming from Hollywood or the Sunset Strip and headed west, turn right.)

1-4. CELEBRITY HOUSES ON HILLCREST DRIVE

On this street, north of Sunset, you can see the last homes of comedian and character actor Morey Amsterdam, who played Buddy on "The Dick Van Dyke Show" (1012 Hillcrest Drive), and comedian Groucho Marx (1083 Hillcrest Drive).

If you continue north past Wallace Ridge, you can also see, at 1174 Hillcrest, the split-level French-regency style house that Elvis Presley bought in May 1967 shortly after his marriage to Priscilla. Elvis did not live in that house for very long. A few months after buying this house, he decided he wanted to buy a home that afforded more privacy, and moved to 144 Monovale Drive, the last of several homes in which he lived in Los Angeles. That last home, which is featured later in this tour, is probably the more interesting of the two.

Comedian Danny Thomas lived in a mansion he called Villa Roisa at 1187 Hillcrest Drive, which is at the end of the street; and it was there, on May 21, 1980, that his daughter Marlo married talk show host Phil Donahue. The best place to view the Thomas estate, though, is not from up close, but from a distance on Wallace Ridge.

Instead of continuing on Hillcrest, make a left turn onto Wallace Ridge and stop around 1120 Wallace Ridge, a pink mansion that the rock star Prince once lived in and which tour guides still point out as his. If you look to your left you can see Thomas' home from across the ravine. It is the last home on the right of the mountain.

After viewing Thomas' estate, continue down Wallace Ridge and make a left onto Loma Vista Drive.

5. GREYSTONE MANSION, 905 Loma Vista Drive

This magnificent 55-room mansion, built in 1923, was the largest and most expensive home in Beverly Hills in the 1920s. It was built by oilman Edward Doheny—the same Edward Doheny who was embroiled in the Teapot Dome scandal. Doheny, who was not content with his personal fortune of $100,000,000, was accused of paying President Warren G. Harding's Secretary of the Interior, Albert Fall, a $100,000 bribe in return for secret leases to government oil reserves at Elk Hills and Buena Vista in California. His trial ended in an acquittal. In 1928 Doheny built the mansion as a gift for his only son, Edward Jr., who moved in with his wife and children. A few weeks later, however, Edward Jr. and his male secretary, Hugh Plunkett, were both found dead in Doheny's bedroom, giving rise to unconfirmed rumors that they died in a lovers' quarrel.

Edward Jr.'s widow continued to live at Greystone until 1955, when Henry Crown, the owner of the Empire State Building, paid $25 million for the estate and subdivided it. What remained of the property was subsequently leased to the American Film Institute, and is now a public park owned and operated by the city of Beverly Hills.

If you stop at Greystone, do not be surprised to see movie crews. The mansion and grounds have frequently been used as a movie location, and the films *Ghostbusters* (where it was used as Gracie Mansion), *All of Me, The Witches of Eastwick, The Bodyguard, Indecent Proposal,*

Guilty by Suspicion, The Fabulous Baker Boys, The Marrying Man, Death Becomes Her, Nixon, and *The Beautician and the Beast* have all filmed here. So have television programs such as "Dynasty," "Falcon Crest," and "Knots Landing."

(DIRECTIONS: After leaving Greystone, make a right turn onto Loma Vista Drive and then another right onto Doheny Drive.)

6. MERV GRIFFIN'S FORMER HOME, 603 N. Doheny Drive (northwest corner of Schuyler Road)

(DIRECTIONS: After seeing Merv's former home, continue on Doheny Drive, then make a left turn onto Foothill Road.)

7. HOME OWNED BY FRANK SINATRA, 915 Foothill Drive

Frank Sinatra owns the mansion at 915 Foothill Drive. Former Universal Studios chairman Lew Wasserman lived in the $8 million home next door at 911 Foothill Drive.

(DIRECTIONS: Make a right at Sunset Boulevard, and continue going west three blocks until you see the sign that says: "Beverly Drive/Crescent Drive." The Beverly Hills Hotel is just past Crescent Drive.)

8. BEVERLY HILLS HOTEL AND BUNGALOWS, 9641 Sunset Boulevard, (310) 276-2251; (800) 283-8885

The Beverly Hills Hotel is one of the most famous hotels in the world. It was built by developer Burton Green in 1912, and it is often said that almost every one of the richest, most powerful, or most famous people on earth has stayed here at one time or another. Some members of Britain's royal family consider it a home away from home. Famous American guests include the extraordinarily eccentric billionaire Howard Hughes, who stayed at the hotel off and on for almost thirty years, even though he owned several houses in Los Angeles during that time. According to the hotel's press kits, Hughes was known to order roast beef sandwiches and then require the hotel staff to hide them in trees for him. Hughes had one of his nervous breakdowns in Bungalow 4.

Bungalow 5 is favored by former *TV Guide* publisher Walter Annenberg, who stays at the hotel for five to six weeks every summer. Marilyn Monroe reportedly had affairs with John and Robert Kennedy in other bungalows, and Elizabeth Taylor shared bungalows there with six of her first seven husbands (Nicky Hilton, who owned his own hotels, was reportedly the lone exception).

The hotel's celebrated Polo Lounge has been described by the *Los Angeles Times* "as much a stage and an office where entertainment industry executives make deals as it is a restaurant . . . [It is] the best improvisational theater in town."

The hotel is owned by the Sultan of Brunei, who, according to *Fortune* magazine, is the richest person in the world. The Sultan paid $185 million for the hotel in 1987, $50 million more than previous owner Marvin Davis paid.

Rates for one-bedrooms start at $275 a night.

9-12. CELEBRITY HOMES ON BEVERLY DRIVE

On each of the streets surrounding the Beverly Hills Hotel you can see some of the most impressive estates in Beverly Hills. In fact, it almost does not matter

In Beverly Hills, even the mailboxes are special.

The Beverly Hills Hotel.

which direction you proceed from here. There is something worth seeing in virtually every direction.

When you approach the hotel from Sunset Boulevard, the sign that reads "Beverly Drive/Crescent Drive," will alert you to the fact that there are actually two streets on the east side of the hotel. Some of the organized tours, as they approach the hotel from Sunset Boulevard, make an immediate right at Beverly Drive; others make a far right turn at Crescent Drive, where Gloria Swanson and Milton Berle lived at 904 and 908 N. Crescent Drive, respectively. If Swanson's and Berle's former homes interest you, make a right turn from Sunset onto Crescent, and then a left at the first street, Lexington Drive. You will wind up at the exact same location as if you had made a right turn onto Beverly Drive.

From Sunset Boulevard, make a right turn onto Beverly Drive, a street that was once owned in its entirety by Beverly Hills' first mayor, humorist and silent film star Will Rogers. Rogers had a home at 925 N. Beverly until about 1928, when he moved to Pacific Palisades (see page 76). Singer Pat Boone still lives at 904 Beverly Drive. Carolyn Jones, who played Morticia in the television series "The Addams Family," lived at 907 Beverly, and "M*A*S*H" star Wayne Rogers lived at 916 Beverly.

If you continue north on Beverly Drive, Beverly will turn into Coldwater Canyon Drive, one of the major thoroughfares connecting Beverly Hills with the San Fernando Valley.

It is possible to take a side trip north on Coldwater Canyon; however, from Beverly, the author recommends taking a left turn onto Lexington Road. Continue half a mile to Hartford Way, make a right on Hartford Way, and then an immediate right to Cove Way, which will lead you to the former home of Sidney Poitier and then the one-time homes of David O. Selznick, Charlie Chaplin, Douglas Fairbanks, Jr. and Mary Pickford, and Sammy Davis, Jr.

13. FORMER HOME OF SIDNEY POITIER, 1007 Cove Way

Poitier, who was the first black actor to win an Oscar (for his performance in *Lillies of the Field*), and one of Hollywood's first black directors, lived in this house for 19 years. In 1994 he sold the house for $4.5 million to a co-chairman of Northwest Airlines.

14. HOME ONCE OWNED BY DAVID O. SELZNICK AND LATER BY ED McMAHON, 1050 Summit Drive (corner of Cove)

This mansion, originally built in the 1930s for *Gone with the Wind* producer David O. Selznick and his wife, Irene Mayer, has had a succession of celebrity owners, including Sammy Davis, Jr. (who later moved a block away); producer Freddie Fields; and Johnny Carson's sidekick Ed McMahon. McMahon sold it in 1991 for $4.1 million as part of his divorce settlement from his wife, Victoria.

15. CHARLIE CHAPLIN'S "BREAKWAY" HOME, 1085 Summit Drive (corner of Cove)

Chaplin's two-story Spanish-style mansion, built in 1922, became famous because everything inside used to fall apart. "To save money on its construction," Charles Lockwood wrote in *Dream Palaces*, an intriguing book about the mansions of Beverly Hills, Chaplin "used studio carpenters when they weren't busy making sets. This seemed like a sensible plan, but it turned out to be a mistake. His carpenters had become so accustomed to

CELEBRITIES WHO LIVE ON COLDWATER CANYON: Jeanne Cooper, Barry Diller, Carrie Fisher, Cuba Gooding, Jr., Charlton Heston, Peter Strauss, Mel Torme and Chuck Woolery. A number of celebrities also live on the various side streets off Coldwater Canyon: Clive Barker, Marilyn Beck, Candice Bergen, Corbin Bernsen, Tom Bosley, Michael Cimino, Joan Collins, Sid Caesar, Susan Dey, Faye Dunaway, Barbara Eden, John Fogerty, Jami Gertz, Woody Harrelson, Gabe Kaplan, Christie McVie, Bette Midler, Theresa Russell, Vidal Sassoon, James Spader, Connie Stevens, Esther Williams, and James Woods.

Another famous resident of the area is comedy director John Landis. Landis' credits include *Kentucky Fried Movie, National Lampoon's Animal House, The Blues Brothers, Trading Places, Spies Like Us, Three Amigos, Coming to America,* and the segment in *The Twilight Zone: The Movie* in which he ordered a helicopter too close to his actors. The helicopter lost control, killing Vic Morrow and two children. After he was acquitted of criminal charges, Landis bought the former Rock Hudson estate at 9402 Beverly Crest Drive. Hudson died in the house in 1985, becoming the first celebrity known to have died of AIDS.

Another public figure who lives off Coldwater Canyon is former Columbia Pictures president and now independent producer, Dawn Steel, who was pictured on the December 1988 cover of *California* magazine for being one of the worst bosses in California. The magazine, which wrote that the Queen of Mean's "snits and verbal abusiveness are the stuff of legend in an industry in which the ability to act like a ten-year-old bully is viewed as a mark of professionalism," repeated a story that Steel supposedly once told a prospective employee: "'Look, I've gone through hundreds of secretaries . . . I'm hard on them. The last one left just because I called her a c***. Would that be a problem for you?' The woman reportedly said yes and left." Steel's defenders were quick to point out that she was no more abusive than any of Hollywood's top male bosses. Steel's friend and colleague, the late producer Don Simpson, who, according to one estimate, went through 20 to 30 assistants in a three-year period, DreamWorks co-founder Jeffrey "Beat 'em Up" Katzenberg, and former Fox Chairman Barry "Killer" Diller were also cited as the toughest people to work for.

Perhaps the biggest surprise celebrity resident of this area is Watergate conspirator John Dean. Dean, a former aide to President Richard Nixon, implicated Nixon in the cover-up of the 1972 burglary at Democratic National Headquarters in Washington, D.C., and was the man primarily responsible for bringing down the Nixon presidency.

putting together temporary sets that they had forgotten how to build a permanent structure. No sooner had Charlie moved into his new house than little things began to go wrong. Paneling split. Ornamental trim fell to the floors. Doors came loose on their hinges. Floors started to squeak. To Charlie's chagrin, his friends and neighbors began calling his Summit Drive dream palace Breakaway House."

After Chaplin sold the house in 1950, it passed through several hands, and at one point was owned by actor George Hamilton, who according to some, served as a front man for his friends, the Marcoses of the Philippines. Hamilton later sold the house to the daughter of former Saudi arms dealer Adnan Khashoggi. In 1991 the Republic of the Philippines successfully sued to get title of the house, and it was later sold to a private individual.

16. PICKFAIR, 1143 Summit Drive

Pickfair was the most famous house in Hollywood in the 1920s and 1930s, when it was owned by superstars Mary Pickford and Douglas Fairbanks, Sr. Charles Lockwood, in *Dream Palaces*, noted that even though "other stars' dream palaces would be architecturally more distinguished, more expensive, and even larger than Pickfair . . . no one star's home ever claimed the same feverish public devotion year after year. Douglas Fairbanks and Mary Pickford were two of Hollywood's biggest and most enduring stars, and they were the nation's most popular couple. Pickfair was the most famous house in America, even more famous than the White House. More Americans cared about what happened there than at Warren G. Harding or Calvin Coolidge's White House."

After the couple divorced in 1936, Fairbanks moved out, and Pickford's next husband, Buddy Rogers, moved in. According to Pickford's biographer Scott Eyeman, Pickford tried "to donate the property to a charity, university or hospital after her death [in 1971], but the $300,000-$400,000 yearly upkeep dissuaded those who were approached."

In 1979 the house was sold to Los Angeles Lakers' owner Jerry Buss for $5,362,000. Buss, in turn, sold the 42-room mansion to singer Pia Zadora and her multimillionaire husband, Meshulam Riklis, for just under $7 million. Pia promptly demolished Pickfair, much to the horror of Beverly Hills preservationists, and built a new three-story, $10 million mansion on the site.

Less than a year after settling in, Pia divorced Riklis, moved into one of the four other houses the couple owned in the area, and left Riklis alone in the house.

17. LAST HOME OF SAMMY DAVIS, JR., 1151 Summit Drive (across from Pickfair)

(DIRECTIONS: Bear left around Pickfair. Ignore the street sign, which will only confuse you—Summit turns into Pickfair—and then make a left onto San Ysidro Drive.)

18. LAST HOME OF FRED ASTAIRE, 1155 San Ysidro Drive

Go slowly or you will miss it. Astaire's was the first home on your right.

19. LAST HOME OF DANNY KAYE, 1103 San Ysidro Drive

Further down the street; before the intersection of San Ysidro and Tower Road. Kaye's neighbors, Laurence Olivier and Vivien Leigh, lived at 1107 San Ysidro Drive.

(DIRECTIONS: Make a right turn onto Tower Road. Just after 1122 Tower Road, you will come to a three-way intersection with Tower Lane on the left, Tower Grove Drive straight ahead, and Tower Road on the right. Tower Lane is a private road on which Bruce Springsteen has a $13.9 million estate; it is not visible from the street.

Tower Grove features an extraordinary French chateau at 1400 Tower Grove, which was once the site of a house owned by a succession of entertainment figures, including David O. Selznick and Elton John, and some historically interesting houses such as the site of John Barrymore's home, Bella Vista, which was also later lived in by Katherine Hepburn, Marlon Brando, and Candice Bergen. Unfortunately, from this direction, Tower Grove is reachable only by negotiating a very steep mountainous road. The road is guaranteed to make even the most experienced driver skip a few heartbeats.

Unless you are absolutely determined to see Hollywood madam Heidi Fleiss' former home at 1270 Tower Grove Drive, you are probably better off making a right turn onto Tower Road, which dead-ends at the top of a hill which is much easier to negotiate. At the end of Tower Road you can make a U-turn at the cul-de-sac and continue down Tower until you reach Benedict Canyon.)

20-22. CELEBRITY HOMES ON TOWER ROAD

Jack Lemmon lives at 1143 Tower Road; Jay Leno lived at 1151; and Sid Sheinberg, the former president and chief operating officer of Universal Studios lives in the former Spencer Tracy estate at 1158 Tower Road.

(DIRECTIONS: After touring Tower Road and turning around you will reach Benedict Canyon. At this point you can either make a right turn and see Harold Lloyd's estate, Green Acres; what you can see of the Manson murder site; and the house that George "Superman" Reeves died in; and then make a U-turn again. Or you can skip these houses and make a left turn from Tower Road and proceed to the $47.5 million mansion owned by David Geffen, the richest man in Hollywood, and then proceed to Roxbury Drive, where Lucille Ball and other celebrities lived. The following descriptions should help you decide which option to choose.)

23. GREEN ACRES, 1740 Green Acres Drive

This 48,000 square-foot mansion, complete with 44 rooms and 26 bathrooms, was sold by producer and Marshall Field heir Ted Field in 1993 for nearly $18 million. From the street all you can see are one of the twelve fountains. Not visible are the twelve formal gardens, the 120-foot-long cascading waterfall, the Olympic-size swimming pool, and the 800-foot-long canoe pond lake near the 9-hole golf course (which is adjacent to the 9-hole golf course on the former Jack Warner estate. The two courses were sometimes combined whenever the owners wanted to play a full 18 holes.) Green Acres was built by silent film star Harold Lloyd, who lived in the mansion for more than 40 years until his death in 1971.

24. SITE OF THE CHARLES MANSON CULT MURDERS, 10048 Cielo Drive

One of the most savage and well publicized murders ever committed in the United States occurred here on the early morning hours of August 9, 1969. Four members of Charles Manson's cult cut telephone lines, climbed a rocky hillside, broke into the main house and slaughtered actress Sharon Tate (who was eight and a half months pregnant with director Roman Polanski's baby); coffee heiress Abigail Folger; Folger's lover, producer Wojtek Frykowski; internationally known hair stylist Jay Sebring; and Steven Parent, an 18-year-old college student who happened to be visiting the estate's caretaker. Tate was stabbed 16 times, and Frykowski 51 times. The murderers wrote the word "Pig" on the wall of the house with the victims' blood.

Manson supposedly ordered his cult followers to kill the house's occupants because he wanted to terrify Doris Day's son, record producer Terry Melcher, whom

Manson had asked to help further his (Manson's) recording career. Until a few months before the slaughter, Melcher had lived in the house with his then-girlfriend Candice Bergen. After Melcher moved out, Tate and her husband, director Roman Polanski, rented the house.

Even today, the murder is relived on television tabloid shows, and Manson is held up as an example of Evil personified. The house, high on the hill, was never visible from the street and was in fact torn down in 1994 when the new owners built a 17,000-square foot Mediterranean villa on the site. Tourists can only see the hillside Manson's followers had to scale in order to reach their victims.

To confuse sightseers, the new owners changed the address of the site from 10050 to 10048 Cielo Drive.

The home where the Manson cult killed actress Sharon Tate and four others.

25. FALCON LAIR, 1436 Bella Drive

Falcon Lair was Rudolph Valentino's hideaway and was named for a never-filmed screenplay, *The Hooded Falcon*, written for him by his second wife, Natacha Rambova. According to John Pashdag, author of *Hollywoodland USA*: "When Valentino bought the house in 1925, his popularity was such that the high wall alone couldn't keep out the female fans, so the screen's first great Latin lover added floodlights, guards, and half a dozen dogs, including three Great Danes and two mastiffs, to keep his admirers at bay."

Tobacco heiress Doris Duke, who was one of the richest women in the world, lived in the house from 1953 until her death in 1993.

26. "SUPERMAN" DEATH HOUSE, 1579 Benedict Canyon Drive

George Reeves, who was television's "Superman" from 1952 to 1957, was found dead in his home in the early hours of June 16, 1959, with a .30 caliber Luger by his side. His death was officially ruled a suicide; however, his mother never accepted the official ruling and hired private detectives in an unsuccessful attempt to prove he was murdered. Some writers later claimed that Reeves' ghost haunts the house. The fact that a subsequent owner, screenwriter/director Phil Robinson, was inspired here to write the ghost story, *Field of Dreams*, is probably just a coincidence.

27. DAVID GEFFEN'S MANSION, 1801 Angelo Drive (just west of Benedict Canyon)

Geffen, who founded DreamWorks, Hollywood's newest studio, along with Steven Spielberg and Jeffrey Katzenberg, is consistently rated by the entertainment

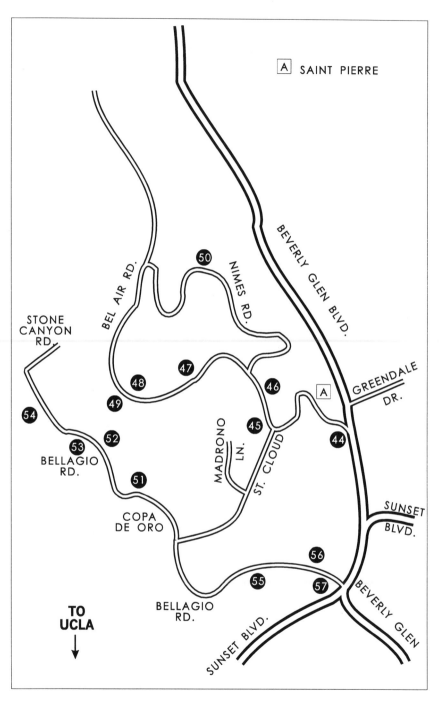

MAP 5   BEL - AIR

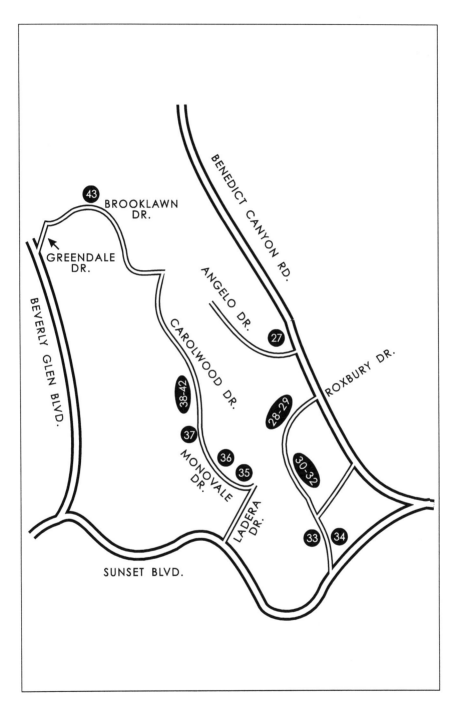

MAP 4   BEVERLY HILLS

OTHER CELEBRITIES WHO LIVE ON BENEDICT CANYON: Jacqueline Bissett, Alan Carr, Kenny G, Martin Lawrence, Ann-Margret and Roger Smith, Darren McGavin, Hugh O'Brien, Julia Phillips, Alfonso Ribeiro, Rita Rudner, Ridley Scott, Gene Simmons and Shannon Tweed, and Ed Zwick. Unfortunately, virtually all of these houses are not visible from the street, which is why no organized tour covers the street.

Several celebrities also live on the many side streets off Benedict Canyon, including Barry Bostwick, Richard Dawson, Mary Frann, Mary Hart, Angelica Huston, Martin Landau, Robert Loggia, Jeff Lynne, Tom Snyder, and Stephanie Powers.

Former residents of Benedict Canyon include Mickey Rourke, whose lost his house at 1020 Benedict Canyon in a foreclosure; Eddie Murphy, who lived in a house he bought from Cher at 2727 Benedict Canyon before moving permanently to the East Coast; Humphrey Bogart and Lauren Bacall, who lived at 2707 Benedict Canyon between 1946 and 1952; Belinda Carlyle; Donna Mills; and the late MacDonald Carey and Elizabeth Montgomery.

magazines as one of the most powerful men in Hollywood. He spent $47.5 million for this estate, which was once owned by Warner Bros. co-founder Jack Warner. When Geffen bought it from Warner's widow he paid the highest price ever paid for a private home in the United States. Behind the gates, the house reportedly looks like Versailles, but unfortunately from the street, only the half-block-long walls can be seen.

(DIRECTIONS: From Benedict Canyon, make a right turn onto Roxbury Drive.)

28. LAST HOME OF AGNES MOORHEAD, 1023 Roxbury Drive
Moorhead played Elizabeth Montgomery's mother on "Bewitched."

29. FORMER HOME OF GEORGE AND IRA GERSHWIN, 1019 Roxbury Drive
Two doors down, at 1019 Roxbury Drive, is a house that lyricists George and Ira Gershwin leased when they moved to Los Angeles in the late 1930s. George died of a brain tumor in 1937, but Ira stayed there, until moving next door to 1021 Roxbury Drive, where the Gershwin family's Roxbury Recordings was based.

1019 Roxbury Drive was later owned by the late Jose Ferrer and his former wife, the popular singer Rosemary Clooney. Rosemary is the aunt of *Batman* and "ER" star George Clooney, and when George first moved to Los Angeles to try his luck as an actor in the early 1980s, he lived here with his aunt for a while.

30. HOME OF PETER FALK, 1004 Roxbury Drive
The actor is best known for his portrayal of the Los Angeles police detective, Lieutenant Columbo. His portrayal has earned him four Emmy Awards.

31. FORMER HOME OF JACK BENNY, 1002 Roxbury Drive
Jack Benny lived next door to Falk's current residence for almost thirty years. In 1966 he moved into an apartment, and then to his last residence, a mansion across from the Playboy Mansion (see page 55).

32. LAST HOME OF LUCILLE BALL, 1000 Roxbury Drive (corner of Lexington)

In 1955 Lucy paid $85,500 for the house. Lucy died in 1989 and three years later, the house was sold for $3.7 million.

The photograph shown below depicts the house as it appeared in 1992. The new owners completely remodeled it, leaving only the original walls standing.

33. FORMER HOME OF RICK SCHRODER, 918 Roxbury Drive

The former star of "Silver Spoons" now lives in a ranch in Colorado with his wife Andrea.

Lucy's house on Roxbury Drive.

34. HOME OF JIMMY STEWART, 921 Roxbury Drive

Stewart still lives in this house, which he moved to after marrying his late wife Gloria in 1949.

(DIRECTIONS: At the end of the block is Sunset Boulevard. Make a right turn onto Sunset and continue west for about half a mile. Make a right onto Ladera Drive, and an immediate left onto Monovale Drive.)

35. HOME AT 120 MONOVALE DRIVE (corner of Ladera and Monovale Drives)

This was Frank Sinatra and Mia Farrow's honeymoon home. They lived here for a short time in 1966.

36. ELVIS PRESLEY'S LAST LOS ANGELES HOME, 144 Monovale Drive

Elvis lived here, next door to 120 Monovale Drive, from December 1967 to March 1975, when he sold the house to "Kojak" star Telly Savalas. About all that is visible from the street is Elvis' former balcony.

(Note: In what seems like a conspiracy to confuse tourists, Monovale Drive changes its name and becomes Carolwood Drive at this point.)

37. HOUSE FORMERLY OWNED BY "BEATLE" GEORGE HARRISON, DAN ROWAN, AND BURT REYNOLDS, 245 Carolwood Drive

Burt Reynolds used his profits from the *Smokey and the Bandit* movies to buy this Mediterranean-style home in the mid-1980s. He lived there with his former wife, Loni Anderson, until 1990. The home was earlier owned by Dan Rowan, co-star of "Rowan and Martin's

Laugh-in," and before that by George Harrison of the Beatles.

Ironically (from the outside, at least), tourists may be more impressed with the two houses next door, owned by ordinary multimillionaires, at 265 and 275 Monovale Drive. These houses sport some of the most modern statues in the city.

38-42. "CELEBRITY ROW": 301 TO 375 CAROL-WOOD DRIVE

Celebrities also seemed to cluster along the rest of this block. Barbra Streisand, who now lives in a three-home compound in Malibu, made 301 Carolwood Drive her primary residence between 1969 and 1997.

A noncelebrity lives at 325 Carolwood, but next door to that—at 355 Carolwood—is the home that Walt Disney lived in until his death in 1966.

Next door—at 375 Carolwood—is the longtime home of film legend Gregory Peck.

At the end of the block—at 391 Carolwood, where the Dobermans bark the loudest and the barbed wire looks the most menacing—is Rod Stewart's former home. In 1992 the popular rock star moved to a gated community on Mulholland Drive.

(DIRECTIONS: Make a left at Brooklawn Drive and proceed 1/10 of a mile.)

43. "THE COLBYS" MANSION, 1060 Brooklawn Drive

The exterior of this house, owned by Hilton Hotels CEO Barron Hilton, was used as "The Colbys" residence in the "Dynasty" spin-off of that name. The house is not visible from the street.

(DIRECTIONS: Brooklawn changes its name to North Faring. As you continue, you will see on your left Harvard/Westlake School, an exclusive private preparatory school which counts among its graduates Candice Bergen, Shirley Temple, Tori Spelling, Bridget Fonda, Tracy Nelson, Sally Ride, and June Lockhart. At the stop sign, make a right turn at Greendale Drive. Then make a left onto Beverly Glen Boulevard, and an immediate right at St. Pierre Road.)

44. ONE-TIME RESIDENCE OF JOHNNY "TARZAN" WEISMULLER, 414 St. Pierre Road

Tour guides often point out the 150-foot long swimming pool which resembles a moat. Weismuller swam there daily, but he did have it built. According to Elaine Young, the realtor to the stars, the pool was actually built by the original owner who wanted to propose to his fiance on a gondola.

Another little-known fact about the mansion is that Mick Jagger of the Rolling Stones rented this house in 1972 when he needed an L.A. base to rehearse for a U.S. tour. John Phillips of the Mamas and The Papas had recommended the house, and Phillips later rented it himself and hosted some wild parties for his friends. In his autobiography *Papa John*, Phillips admitted he was evicted for nonpayment of rent.

(Note: St. Pierre changes its name to St. Cloud Road here.)

45. FORMER HOME OF SONNY AND CHER, 364 St. Cloud Road

In the 1991 remake of *Father of the Bride*, Steve Martin had some comic scenes here when he sneaked into his wealthy in-laws' study and tried to see their bank book. In real life the estate was once owned by Sonny and Cher, who sold it to another former owner, *Hustler* magazine publisher Larry Flynt. In *The People vs. Larry Flynt,* the mansion was featured briefly for a scene in which Woody Harrelson, playing Flynt, was taken into custody by federal marshals.

46. FORMER JOHNNY CARSON HOME, 400 St. Cloud Road

Carson bought this house in 1972 from Mervyn LeRoy, the producer of *The Wizard of Oz,* and lived here until 1983. It is now occupied by Carson's ex-wife number three, Joanna.

(DIRECTIONS: Bear to the left when you reach the intersection without a sign.)

47. RONALD REAGAN'S RETIREMENT HOME, 668 St. Cloud Road

Reagan's wealthy friends bought this house for him before he left office and gave him a three-year lease with an option to buy. The address was originally 666 St. Cloud, but Nancy Reagan, perhaps after consulting with her astrologer, had the house number changed to 668. 666 is the Sign of the Beast in the Book of Revelations in the New Testament.

(Note: St. Cloud changes names and becomes Bel Air Road without warning.)

48. "BEVERLY HILLBILLIES" MANSION, 750 Bel Air Road

Adjacent to the Reagans' is the house that Jed Clampett and his family called home in "The Beverly

Hillbillies," the enormously popular television show that aired from 1962 to 1970. The mansion was once known as the Kirkeby Estate, and was considered to be one of the great estates of Beverly Hills until it was bought in 1986 by Hollywood dealmaker Jerrold Perrenchio, a former agent of Liz Taylor and Marlon Brando and former partner of television producer Norman Lear. Perrenchio, whose net worth was estimated by *Forbes* magazine to be around $665 million, paid $13.6 million for the mansion, dismantled it, and bought the three neighboring properties for an additional $9 million, in order to build what one writer called "what by all accounts looks to be a modern monument to himself."

49. ANOTHER FORMER "MAMAS AND THE PAPAS" HOUSE, 783 Bel Air Road (corner of Strada Vecchia)

John and Michelle Phillips of the Mamas and the Papas leased this home across the street from the "Beverly Hillbillies" mansion for three years in the late 1960s before moving to the one at 414 St. Pierre Road.

Previous owners include Jeanette MacDonald and Nelson Eddy.

(DIRECTIONS: At the intersection of Bel Air Road and Nimes Road, you can either turn left and see Alfred Hitchcock's last home at 910 Bel Air Road, Zsa Zsa Gabor's home at 1001 Bel Air Road—which, incidentally, was also Howard Hughes' last Los Angeles home—and Art Linkletter's home at 1100 Bel Air Road. Or, you can make a right turn at the intersection and see:)

50. HOME OF ELIZABETH TAYLOR, 700 Nimes Road

Taylor, who has overcome most of her addictions—except her addiction to publicity—lives here, just up the street from the 658 Nimes Road, where composer Burt Bacharach lived for years, and 688 Nimes Road, a home built for Warner Baxter, a one-time leading man whose career spanned from 1914 to 1950. Baxter was Hollywood's top money-earner in 1936. His home was subsequentled owned by Jack Ryan, the inventor of the Barbie doll. Singer-songwriter Mac Davis lives at 759 Nimes Road.

(*DIRECTIONS: Proceed south on Nimes and bear left onto St. Cloud. You will pass 400 and 364 St. Cloud again, as well as 322 St. Cloud, which was once owned by MGM co-founder Louis B. Mayer and later by comedian Jerry Lewis. Just past Madrono Lane, you will see a sign pointing toward the Hotel Bel-Air. The street name is not visible, but that street is Copa De Oro Road. Make a right turn onto Copa De Oro. A block away you will see another sign announcing Amapola Lane. Look to your right. The mammoth white colonial at 420 Amapola Lane is owned by comedian Bob Newhart. Continue on Copa De Oro Road.)*

51. LONG-TIME HOME OF TOM JONES, 363 Copa De Oro Road

The singer bought this red-brick Tudor home from singer-actor Dean Martin in 1976. Jones, who now spends most of his time in England and in Las Vegas, where he performs regularly, recently offered the nine-bedroom, 13,000-square-foot home for sale for just under $8 million.

An aerial view of "The Beverly Hillbillies" home and Ronald Reagan's retirement home next door.

(DIRECTIONS: Make a right turn onto Bellagio Road and then another right onto Stone Canyon Road. On your left you will see Bellagio Road again. Two houses down is 10615 Bellagio Road, the last home of "Star Trek" creator Gene Roddenberry. Cary Grant also lived in that house at one point. You can make a quick left to see the house, but to continue the tour you want to keep heading north on Stone Canyon to the Hotel Bel-Air.)

52. FORMER GREER GARSON ESTATE, 680 Stone Canyon Road

Garson, a popular actress in the 1940s, won an Academy Award for her role in *Mrs. Miniver.* She was nominated for best actress on six other occasions.

53. DON SIMPSON'S LAST HOME, 685 Stone Canyon Road

Simpson was one of the most successful and most disturbed producers in recent motion picture history. With his partner Jerry Bruckheimer, he produced hit after hit in the 1980s and early 1990s, including *Flashdance, Beverly Hills Cop, Top Gun, Days of Thunder, Crimson Tide, Dangerous Minds,* and *The Rock.*

On January 19, 1996, the 52-year-old producer's body was found in an upstairs bathroom of his mansion. Investigators were startled to discover over 2,200 (yes, 2,200) alphabetically arranged pills in a nearby closet. The coroner ruled that he died of heart failure caused by an overdose of cocaine and various prescription medications.

After his death, columnist Marilyn Beck wrote: "Simpson was lionized by hundreds of industry figures as everything from a tremendous storyteller to an unapologetic carouser. He was also a sick man heavily into sadomasochism who reportedly disfigured a prostitute during an S&M encounter."

The bestseller *You'll Never Make Love in This Town Again,* and it sequel, *Once More with Feeling,* documented other Simpson escapades with prostitutes that made this alleged disfigurement almost seem tame by comparison. The accounts are too horrific to repeat here. Even Hollywood madam Heidi Fleiss distanced herself from Simpson, insisting: "I didn't supply him with the kinky girls. Don was Madam Alex's [her rival's] client. Actually her bread and butter."

53. HOTEL BEL-AIR, 701 Stone Canyon Road, (310) 472-1211, (800) 648-4097

Everyone raves about the Hotel Bel-Air. Charles Moore, Peter Becker, and Regula Campbell, in their guide to Los Angeles architectural highlights, *The City Observed,* call it "one of the most wonderful places in Southern California." *Conde Nast Traveler, Forbes* and *USA Today* all rate it as the best city hotel in the United States. Gault Millau's *The Best of Los Angeles* gushes: "If Sleeping Beauty were to wake up in Southern California, no doubt she'd find herself in the enchanted gardens of the Hotel Bel-Air. The grounds are so beautiful that they almost seem to be a fairy-tale parody. You will be charmed by the swans, the ancient trees, the eleven acres of private park, the welcoming reception with its crackling fire and the quasi-country-chateau architecture."

You will also be impressed with the celebrities you will see at the hotel. It is one of the best places in town to see celebrities, visiting European royalty, and traveling industry leaders.

(DIRECTIONS: After leaving the hotel, make a left turn and head south toward Sunset. Stone Canyon leads to Sunset; however, you do not want to go that far since you can only make a right turn at Sunset, which is a very busy street. About 3/10 of a mile past the Hotel Bel-Air, you will reach Bellagio Road again. Make a left, heading east on Bellagio Road. The street signs here are very confusing, so make sure you follow the sign that reads "Sunset Boulevard East", and bear right for a block where you will see a sign announcing the 300 block of Copa De Oro Road. Go on Copa De Oro Road for a block, then make a left at the sign which says 10400 Bellagio Road.)

55. FORMER BRIAN WILSON AND EDGAR RICE BURROUGHS HOUSE, 10452 Bellagio Road

Brian Wilson of the Beach Boys bought this Mediterranean villa, once owned by "Tarzan" creator Edgar Rice Burroughs, in the 1960s, and painted it purple, upsetting the neighborhood homeowners' association to no end.

56. *"9 TO 5"* FILMING SITE, 10431 Bellagio Road

According to John Pashdag, author of *Hollywoodland USA*, this was "Dabney Coleman's house in *9 to 5,* where Jane Fonda, Dolly Parton, and Lily Tomlin tied up their no-good boss, and hung him from the ceiling."

57. HOME AT 10410 BELLAGIO ROAD

Home of St. Louis (and former Los Angeles) Rams' owner Georgia Frontiere.

OTHER CELEBRITIES WHO LIVE IN BEL-AIR: Lindsay Buckingham, Red Buttons, Clint Eastwood, Michael Eisner, Christine Ferrare, Dennis Franz, Lee Iacocca, Quincy Jones, Harvey Korman, Judith Krantz, Dick Martin, Leonard Nimoy, Martha Raye, Della Reese, Frank Robinson, Neil Simon, Jaclyn Smith, Joel Schumacher, Robert Stack, Gene Wilder, Dave Winfield, and Jane Wyatt.

Some tours point out a home on Sunset Boulevard as belonging to Joanne Carson, Johnny's second wife, and note that Truman Capote died in her house. Carson does live on Sunset Boulevard, but she lives in Brentwood, west of UCLA, not in Bel-Air.

Former Bel-Air residents include the late Ted Bessell, W. C. Fields, Clark Gable and Carole Lombard, Judy Garland, Henry Fonda, and Elvis Presley. Presley lived at 565 Perugia Way between 1960 and 1965. He jammed with the Beatles at his home on August 27, 1965. There were rumors that the jam session was recorded. However, the tapes have never surfaced.

(DIRECTIONS: Make a right turn onto Bel Air Road, which will take you to the east gate of the community of Bel-Air. You should recognize the gates; it has been on television often enough. You may have seen it in the opening credits of "The Rockford Files." Continue straight across Sunset Boulevard, where the street changes its name to Beverly Glen. You are now in Holmby Hills, a neighborhood that is even more expensive than Beverly Hills and Bel-Air. Take Beverly Glen Boulevard south for about half a mile; and then by the park—Holmby Park— make a left onto Club View Drive. The first house on the left is the talk of Los Angeles.)

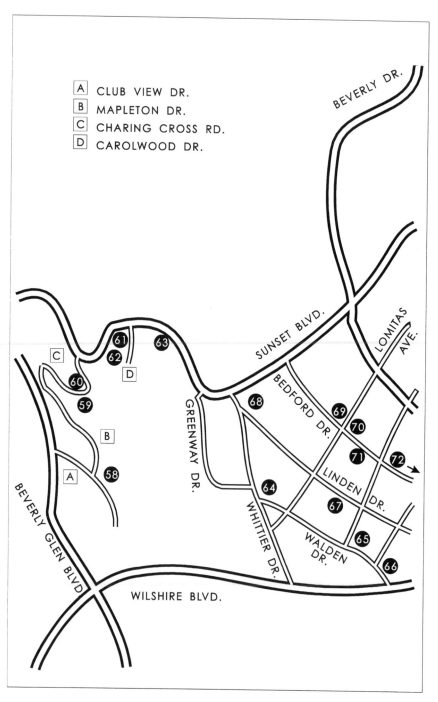

A CLUB VIEW DR.
B MAPLETON DR.
C CHARING CROSS RD.
D CAROLWOOD DR.

BEVERLY DR.

SUNSET BLVD.

LOMITAS AVE.

61
62
63
D
C
60
59
B
A
58

GREENWAY DR.

BEDFORD DR.

68
69
70
71
72

WHITTIER DR.

64
LINDEN DR.
67
65
WALDEN DR.
66

BEVERLY GLEN BLVD

WILSHIRE BLVD.

MAP 6 BEVERLY HILLS

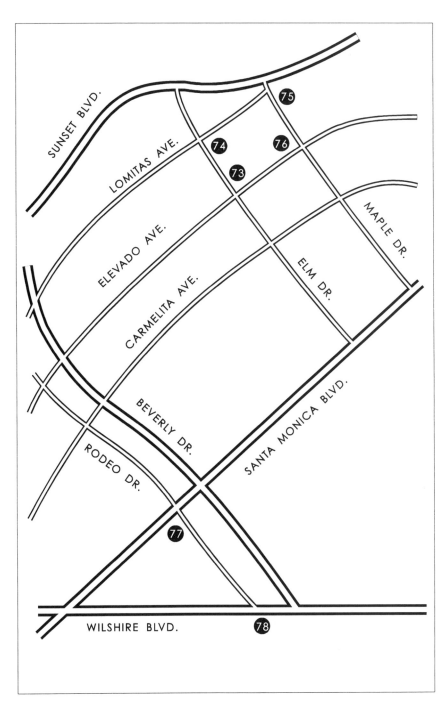

MAP 7 BEVERLY HILLS

Producer Aaron Spelling's home is the largest and most extravagant private residence in Los Angeles.

58. AARON SPELLING'S CHATEAU, 594 N. Mapleton Drive (corner of Club View)

Comedian David Steinberg once remarked: "In Hollywood, there's the rich. And then there's Aaron Spelling." Spelling is not a household name, even though he was honored in the *Guinness Book of World Records* for being the most prolific producer of television programs of all time. Spelling is the man responsible for "The Mod Squad," "Charlie's Angels," "Fantasy Island," "The Love Boat," "Starsky and Hutch," "The Rookies," "Hart to Hart," "Hotel," "T. J. Hooker," "Vegas," "Dynasty," "Melrose Place," "Savannah," "Family," and "Beverly Hills 90210." He once told an interviewer the reason he is so successful is because he gives people what they want: "escape from the harshness of day-to-day life."

In 1983 Spelling created what he called "our Fantasy Island" when he spent $10 million for the old Bing Crosby estate, tore it down, and built a six-acre, 123-room, $40 million mansion that is reportedly as large as a football field, or 31 times the size of the average American home. The *Los Angeles Herald Examiner* placed the 56,000-square-foot chateau in perspective by noting it was smaller than the Pentagon, but larger than the Taj Mahal, Disney's largest soundstage, or George Washington's Mt. Vernon home. The dressing room and closets of Spelling's wife, Candy, reportedly take up an entire wing. Even some of Spelling's neighbors think the size of the house is obscene. Not counting the household help, three people live in this house: Aaron, Candy, and their actor son Randy. Their daughter Tori, who played Donna on "Beverly Hills 90210," moved out into a three-bedroom apartment in Westwood.

(DIRECTIONS: After ooh-ing and aah-ing the Spelling Manor, continue north on Mapleton Drive, passing Charing Cross Road, until you see 232 S. Mapleton Drive. That is the former home of Humphrey Bogart and Lauren Bacall, now owned by producer Ray Stark. Make a U-turn as soon as possible and go left onto Charing Cross Road.)

59. THE PLAYBOY MANSION, 10236 Charing Cross Road

Hefner lives and works out of his six-acre estate, which he purchased in 1971.

The Playboy Mansion.

60. FORMER JACK BENNY ESTATE, 10231 Charing
Cross Road

The comedian lived here, in this house directly
across the street from the Playboy Mansion, from 1965
until his death in 1974. The house was later owned by
psychologist, author *(Nice Girls Do)*, and television
personality, Irene Kassorla, and her husband Norman
Friedman, the president of Daisy Systems Corporation.

(DIRECTIONS: Make a right onto Sunset, and proceed
2/10 of mile to Carolwood Drive.

61. JAYNE MANSFIELD'S "PINK PALACE", 10100
Sunset Boulevard

This pink 30-room mansion, now owned by
Englebert Humperdinck, was originally built by Rudy
Vallee and was later owned by sex symbol Jayne
Mansfield. Charles Lockwood, in his book *Dream
Palaces*, reports that "though Jayne may have looked and
acted the part of the dumb blonde, in remodeling the Pink
Palace she knew how to get the most for her money. Her
Hungarian muscleman husband, Mickey Hargitay, had
been a builder, and he completed or supervised most of the
work. Then Jayne's press agent, Jim Byron, asked fifteen
hundred furniture and building supply houses for free
samples. Think of the honor, he told them, of having
your—fill in the blank—as part of the Pink Palace. The
pitch worked. Jayne received over a hundred fifty
thousand dollars' worth of free merchandise."

62. OWLWOOD, 141 S. Carolwood Drive

This house, directly behind the Pink Palace on the
cul-de-sac south of Sunset, had a succession of celebrity
owners: Sonny and Cher, Tony Curtis, and 20th Century

Fox co-founder Joseph Schenck. Marilyn Monroe lived here in 1949 when she was Schenck's mistress.

63. HADERWAY HALL, 10000 Sunset Boulevard

The lifelike sculptures in front of this estate have always intrigued tourists. One of the pieces—a couple with binoculars trying to see what is in the houses—leads one to ask if anyone famous ever lived here. The answer is yes. Howard Hughes owned it at one time, and Judy Garland rented the property in 1948. Two years later, when she was separated from her second husband, director Vincente Minnelli, she recuperated from a suicide attempt here.

The statue of a cop giving a ticket to trespassers at the front gate should be self-explanatory, but one can only guess at what the statues of the two naked boys trying to peer over the fence, next to the security cameras, are supposed to represent.

(DIRECTIONS: Continue east on Sunset Boulevard for two blocks and make a right turn onto Greenway Drive, where you will see some of the prettiest lawns on the tour. You are now back in Beverly Hills. You will pass Steve Lawrence and Edie Gorme's *home at 820 Greenway Drive, and a house at 813 Greenway that Debbie Reynolds once owned, and where her daughter, Carrie Fisher, grew up. Producer Blake Edwards and his wife, Julie Andrews, also owned the house at one time.*

At the stop sign make a right turn onto Whittier Drive. Just past the sign on your right that reads Walden Drive is a house on the left side of the three-way corner of Whittier Drive, Lomitas Avenue and Walden Drive. That is Buddy Hackett's house, and you will want to bear left on Walden after his house.)

64. HOME OF BUDDY HACKETT, 800 Whittier Drive

The white elephant in front of his house was reportedly given to him as a gift by his friend Sammy Davis, Jr.

65. HOUSE AT 614 N. WALDEN DRIVE

Several blocks down the street is a house you might recognize from *Beverly Hills Cop II*. Eddie Murphy pretended to be a Beverly Hills building inspector, sent the workmen remodeling it packing, and moved in himself. He told his friends on the Beverly Hills police force that it was his uncle's house.

66. THE WITCH'S HOUSE, 516 N. Walden Drive (corner of Carmelita)

This is perhaps the most unusual house on the tour of Beverly Hills. It looks like the witch's house in "Hansel and Gretel," and although the Beverly Hills Historical Society reports it has not appeared in any famous films, it did appear in some silent films in the 1920s, when the house served as an office for Irvin C. Willat Productions, a movie studio in Culver City. When the studio was sold in 1926, a former owner transplanted the house and moved it to the heart of Beverly Hills. The house was designed by set designer Henry C. Oliver, who won the first Academy Award for art direction for a long-forgotten movie named *Street Angel*.

(DIRECTIONS: At the corner of Walden, make a left onto Carmelita Avenue, and another left onto Linden Drive.)

67. LAST HOME OF DAVID BEGELMAN, 705 Linden Drive

Begelman was the former head of Columbia Pictures who was convicted in 1978 of embezzling company funds. He had forged his signature on several checks, including the one which proved to be his undoing: it was a $10,000 check with actor Cliff Robertson's name on it. The scandal, which was chronicled in David McClintock's bestseller *Indecent Exposure*, did not end Begelman's movie career. He went on to head MGM productions and Gladden Pictures and produced *Weekend at Bernie's, Wisdom, and The Fabulous Baker Boys.* In 1995, Begelman committed suicide just as he was about to lose his home for failing to pay the mortgage.

68. "BUGSY" SIEGEL MURDER SITE, 810 Linden Drive

Benjamin "Bugsy" Siegel—the gangster whom J. Edgar Hoover once called "the most dangerous man in America"—was murdered here in a home leased by his mistress, Virginia Hill. The 41-year-old Siegel was shot shortly before midnight on June 20, 1947, reportedly because the Mafia suspected he was skimming money he had borrowed from them to build the Flamingo Hotel in Las Vegas. Besides being the subject of a 1991 movie starring Warren Beatty and Annette Bening, Siegel's main claim to fame was that he reportedly convinced organized crime to build the first luxury hotel in Las Vegas, where gambling was legal. Some say that Las Vegas was built largely as a consequence of Bugsy's vision. In Los Angeles, he ran most of the mob's gambling and prostitution operations and socialized with movie stars like George Raft. *Time* magazine called him "perhaps the most famous mobster of his era."

The Witch's House in Beverly Hills.

The Beverly Hills home in which Bugsy Siegel was killed.

(Note: The producers of *Bugsy* were not able to get permission to use this house in the movie. The Virginia Hill house seen in the movie is located in Hancock Park.)

(DIRECTIONS: At the end of Linden Drive, make a right onto Sunset Boulevard, and then another right onto Bedford Drive.)

69. "DOWN AND OUT IN BEVERLY HILLS" HOME, 802 N. Bedford Drive

This was the house in which Richard Dreyfuss and Bette Midler lived in *Down and Out in Beverly Hills.* (The inside of the house and the backyard pool area were actually recreated on the Disney back lot.)

70. FORMER HOME OF LANA TURNER, 730 N. Bedford Drive

Between her fourth and fifth marriages, actress Lana Turner was dating a small-time Mafia hood named Johnny Stompanato, who used the alias Johnny Valentine. Turner tried to break off the relationship, and according to the official version, on April 5, 1958, an angry Stompanato threatened to kill or disfigure her. Lana's teenage daughter, Cheryl Crane, grabbed a knife and stabbed him to death in an upstairs bedroom.

Although the killing was later ruled a justifiable homicide, questions were raised as to how a 14-year-old girl could overpower the 175-pound ex-Marine. Suspicious minds wondered whether Turner killed Stompanato herself, and Crane took the blame to save her mother's career. After Turner's death, Eric Root, her hairdresser and escort in late life (after her seventh failed marriage), claimed Lana told him: "I killed the son-of-a-bitch and I'll do it again."

71. FORMER HOME OF COMEDIAN STEVE MARTIN, 721 N. Bedford Drive

72. ONE-TIME HOME OF "THE IT GIRL," CLARA BOW, 512 N. Bedford Drive

Bow was considered the Madonna of her day (the Roaring '20s) and had quite a wild reputation. One of Hollywood's favorite legends is that she was so promiscuous that she had sex with the entire starting lineup of the USC football team. Her principal biographer, David Stenn, however, disputes the story. In *Clara Bow*, Stenn writes that Clara was just an avid football fan who used to invite the USC players and their opponents to parties at her house after the games on Saturday nights. The parties were also attended by her actress friends, including Joan Crawford. Lowry McCaslin, a sophomore end for the team, was quoted as saying: "We had a good time, but it wasn't that exciting."

(DIRECTIONS: After viewing Bow's house, make a right turn on to Carmelita Avenue. To see the next major concentration of show-business homes, pass Camden, Rodeo, Beverly, Canon, Crescent, Rexford, Alpine, and Foothill Drives, until you reach Elm Drive.

It should be noted in passing, though, that each of these streets has something to offer of interest. For example, a right on Camden Drive will take you to All Saints Church of Beverly Hills at 504 N. Camden Drive, where funeral services were held for Humphrey Bogart, Alfred Hitchcock and Rudolph Valentino; Rod Stewart married Rachel Hunter; Elizabeth Taylor married the first of her eight husbands; and Dudley Moore first glimpsed Bo Derek in the movie 10. A left onto Rodeo Drive will take you to the late Gene Kelly and Carl Reiner's homes at 714 and 725 Rodeo Drive, respectively. Rodeo Drive going south leads to the world-famous shopping district, usually referred to as Rodeo Drive.

A right on either Crescent or Rexford, going south, leads to the magnificent Beverly Hills City Hall. Alpine is the street that the late comedian Phil Silvers lived on. Author Jackie Collins and director Richard Benjamin live on Foothill Drive.)

73. FORMER HOME OF IVAN REITMAN, 704 N. Elm Drive

Reitman produced and directed numerous blockbuster comedies, including *Kindergarten Cop, Dave, Junior, Ghostbusters, Ghostbusters II, Twins, Legal Eagles, Meatballs* and *Stripes.*

74. REAL LIFE "NIGHTMARE ON ELM DRIVE" HOME, 722 N. Elm Drive

One of Hollywood's most notorious murders occurred here on the night of August 20, 1989, when Jose Menendez, the 45-year-old chairman of Live Entertainment, a division of Carolco Pictures, and his 44-year-old wife Kitty were found brutally slain in their family room. At first police believed that Jose and Kitty might have been killed by mobsters. However, several months later, their two sons, Lyle and Erik, were arrested after confessing to their psychiatrist that they were the killers. (The only reason the brothers were caught was because they also threatened to kill the psychiatrist if he violated doctor-patient confidentiality. The frightened shrink had his mistress—not his wife—eavesdrop on the therapy sessions in case he became their third victim. The mistress took it upon herself to report the brothers' confessions to the Beverly Hills police.)

At both their 1993 trials, in which the brothers were tried separately, and their joint 1996 retrial, the brothers admitted shotgunning their parents, but claimed they were driven to do so because Jose sexually and psychologically tortured them. The defense worked at the original trials (both juries were hung) but failed in the retrial. The brothers were convicted of first-degree murder and conspiracy to commit murder. They were sentenced to life imprisonment with no possibility of parole.

The home had an interesting history even before the Menendez family bought it. It had previously been rented to Elton John, the singer formerly known as Prince, and theatrical producer Hal Prince. The immediate previous owners were Mark Slotkin and his ex-wife, Robin Greer, who were friends with O. J. and Nicole Simpson. In 1985, before O. J. and Nicole's daughter, Sydney, was born, Robin hosted a baby shower for Nicole at the house. Although not a hooker herself, Robin subsequently gained notoriety as one of the four co-authors of the bestselling call girl tell-all *You'll Never Make Love in This Town Again*.

75. LAST HOME OF GEORGE BURNS, 720 N. Maple Drive

The facade of Burns' home was used in the 1950s CBS comedy, "The Burns and Allen Show." Both Burns, who lived in the house for 60 years, and his wife, Gracie Allen, died in this home (Burns in 1996 at the age of 100; Gracie in 1964).

76. FORMER HOME OF DIANA ROSS, 701 N. Maple Drive

77. RODEO DRIVE AND NEARBY BEVERLY HILLS SHOPPING DISTRICT

As one storeowner put it: "You'll see more Rolls Royces on Rodeo Drive in ten minutes than you'll see in Cleveland, Ohio all year."

If you would like to tour this ultrachic shopping district, contact the Beverly Hills Visitors' Bureau and ask for their guide to the stores and their publication, "A Guide to Beverly Hills," which includes a walking tour. The Visitors' Bureau (310-271-8174; 800-345-2210) is very helpful and offers a variety of services, including an Ambassadear program which offers multilingual docents who will host parties, take you on shopping tours, and treat you like a celebrity.

For those who wish to spend some time in the shopping district, there are a number of notable restaurants in the Beverly Hills shopping district which attract a celebrity clientele, including Spago Beverly Hills, 176 N. Canon Drive, (310) 385-0880; The Grill, 9562 Dayton Way, (310) 276-0615; Mr. Chow, 344 N. Camden Drive, (310) 278-9911; and Nate 'n' Al's Delicatessen, 414 N. Beverly Drive, (310) 274-0101. Maple Drive Restaurant, which also attracts entertainment notables, is located just south of Wilshire Boulevard at 345 N. Maple Drive. For reservations call (310) 274-9800.

Except when special events are held, celebrities avoid the Planet Hollywood restaurant, 9560 Wilshire Boulevard, precisely because it attracts ogling tourists. The restaurant is notable, though, as sort of a Hollywood memorabilia museum. In addition to its wall of celebrity handprints, Planet Hollywood displays Sharon Stone's ice pick from *Basic Instinct*, the actual title vehicle from John Ford's classic western *Stagecoach*, costumes that Clark

Gable and Vivien Leigh wore in *Gone with the Wind*, and *Forrest Gump*'s box of chocolates.

79. REGENT BEVERLY WILSHIRE HOTEL, 9500 Wilshire Boulevard, (310) 275-5200, (800) 427-4354

Richard Gere and Julia Roberts stayed in the penthouse suite in *Pretty Woman*. (Although the outside of the hotel was used, the interior scenes were actually shot on a Disney sound stage.) Warren Beatty reportedly lived in a rooftop suite (Room 1001) for over a decade.

OFF THE MAP, at 465 N. Beverly Drive (at Little Santa Monica Boulevard) is the Beverly Hills branch of the Museum of Television & Radio. The museum

The Regent Beverly Wilshire Hotel.

offers entertainment exhibits and sponsors seminars with writers, producers, directors, and actors, and other special events. For information call (310) 786-1000.

The Four Seasons Hotel at Beverly Hills, 300 S. Doheny Drive, is another great place for celebrity-watching. Many studios hold their press junkets there, so there is always a chance you will see a familiar face at the hotel's bar or restaurant. (The hotel was also the site of three celebrity marriages: Rod Stewart and Rachel Hunter; Paula Abdul and Brad Beckerman; and Luke Perry and Minnie Sharp).

Also, at the corner of Olympic Boulevard and LeDoux Road, is the intersection where, in 1989, a policeman stopped Zsa Zsa Gabor in her Rolls-Royce. Zsa Zsa slapped the poor cop, resulting in a worldwide publicity, a three-day prison sentence, and one of the few motion picture offers she has received in recent years: a scene slapping a runaway police car in *Naked Gun 2 ½*.

OTHER CELEBRITIES WHO LIVE IN BEVERLY HILLS: Tony Bennett, James Coburn, Danny DeVito and Rhea Perlman, Neil Diamond, Kenneth "Babyface" Edmonds, Fabio, Jeff Foxworthy, Kate Jackson, Janet Leigh, Shari Lewis, Robert Loggia, Priscilla Presley, Don Rickles, Ringo Starr, Sharon Stone, John Tesh and Connie Selleca, Abigail van Buren, Raquel Welch, and Shelley Winters. Casey Kasem, George C. Scott and Sidney Sheldon live in Holmby Hills.

In 1954 Joe DiMaggio and Marilyn Monroe lived for five months at 508 N. Palm Drive, one street east of Maple Drive. It is often referred to as their "Honeymoon Home" and still attracts tourists.

BRENTWOOD

1. NICOLE BROWN SIMPSON/RON GOLDMAN MURDER SITE, 875 N. Bundy Drive

The three-story townhouse owned by O. J. Simpson's ex-wife Nicole became a macabre tourist attraction after she was murdered there on June 12, 1994, along with Ron Goldman, an acquaintance who worked at Brentwood's Mezzaluna restaurant (11750 San Vicente Boulevard). Nicole had dined at the restaurant with her family earlier that evening, and Goldman drove to the condo after he got off work to return to Nicole her mother's eyeglasses, which had been left behind after the dinner.

The condominium is within walking distance of Nicole's previous residence, a house at 325 S. Gretna Greene Way. That was the site of Nicole's infamous 1993 911 call to the police. In that call, Nicole pleaded with police to come to the house before O. J. harmed her, as he had in the past. O. J. reportedly broke down the back door of that residence.

After the murders, Nicole's estate had an extremely difficult time trying to sell the condominium, but eventually a Century City attorney bought it for under just under $600,000. It was reported that he planned to install landscaping, reconfigure the walkway, remove the stairs, and change the address to make it difficult for tourists to recognize the murder scene.

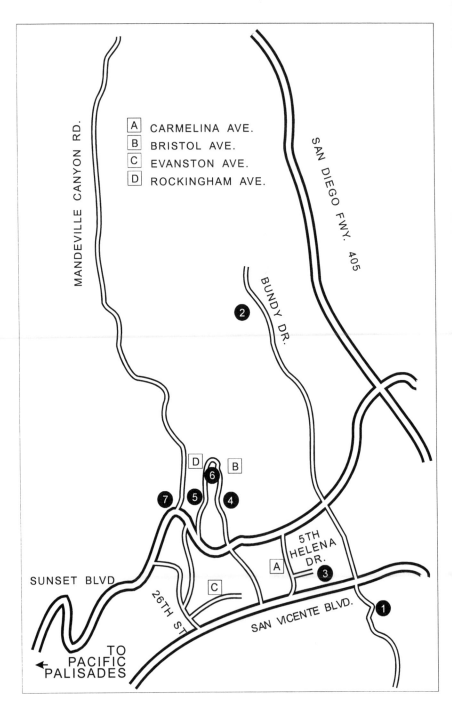

A CARMELINA AVE.
B BRISTOL AVE.
C EVANSTON AVE.
D ROCKINGHAM AVE.

MANDEVILLE CANYON RD.

SAN DIEGO FWY. 405

BUNDY DR.

2

D B
6
7 5 4

5TH HELENA DR.

A

3

SUNSET BLVD

26TH ST

C

SAN VICENTE BLVD.

1

TO
◄ PACIFIC
PALISADES

MAP 8 BRENTWOOD

2. "*SIX CRISES*" HOME, 901 N. Bundy Drive

Richard Nixon leased this house after losing the 1960 presidential election. He wrote *Six Crises* here.

3. MARILYN MONROE HOME, 12305 Fifth Helena Drive (off Carmelina Street)

Although some writers and conspiracy theorists allege that Monroe was murdered here because of her affairs with first John and then Robert Kennedy, Monroe died (at least according to the official autopsy report) of a drug overdose in her bedroom on August 4, 1962. She lived in this house alone with her dog Maf (short for Mafia), which she received as a present from Frank Sinatra.

4. "MOMMIE DEAREST" HOUSE, 426 N. Bristol Avenue

In her book *Mommie Dearest,* Joan Crawford's daughter Christina told of being abused in this house while growing up.

5. SHIRLEY TEMPLE CHILDHOOD HOME, 209 N. Rockingham Avenue

Until 1951, Shirley lived at 209 N. Rockingham, while her parents lived next door at 227 N. Rockingham.

6. O. J. SIMPSON'S MANSION, 360 N. Rockingham Avenue

On June 17, 1994, a suicidal O. J. Simpson surrendered to police in the driveway of his estate after evading arrest earlier that day for the murder of his ex-wife, Nicole Brown Simpson, and her friend, Ronald Goldman. The surrender, which was witnessed by a

Marilyn Monroe died in this Brentwood home.

Roseanne's Evanston Drive home in the early 1990s.

nationally televised audience of 95 million, climaxed an extraordinary day in which Simpson became a fugitive from justice and was chased by police over 60 miles of Southland freeways before returning home. Police had arrested Simpson because investigators had found on his property a bloodstained glove, which matched another glove left at the murder scene, and blood stains in Simpson's driveway and bathroom. At the crime scene, police also found Simpson's blood, a knit cap by Goldman's feet that contained hairs that matched Simpson's, and fibers like those from his car. On Ron Goldman's shirt investigators found Simpson's hairs and fibers that matched his clothing. In his Ford Bronco investigators found a mixture of blood which matched both the victims and Simpson's. Despite this overwhelming circumstantial evidence of guilt, attorneys for the Hall of Fame football player turned sportscaster and actor managed to convince a jury that the evidence was so compromised that Simpson should be acquitted. Sixteen months later, in February 1997, a civil jury determined that Simpson caused Ron and Nicole's deaths.

7. MANDEVILLE CANYON ROAD

This pretty canyon road, just north of Sunset, has always attracted an unusual number of celebrities. Current homeowners include actors John Binder, Cloris Leachman, Julianne Phillips, and superproducers Fred Silverman and Allan Burns. Former residents include Tom Selleck, Mark Harmon and Pam Dawber, Steven Seagal and Kelly LeBrock, Jill Eikenberry and Michael Tucker, directors Barry Levinson and John Badham, and the late Karl Malden, Roy Huggins, and John Candy.

"Bonanza" star Loren Greene lived at 2090 Mandeville Canyon Road for years. Dick Powell once lived on the 3100 block of Mandeville Canyon Road—and a location scout reports that the exterior of his house was used as Robert Wagner and Stephanie Powers' house in the 1979-1984 ABC adventure series "Hart to Hart." It is not, however, visible from the street.

OTHER CELEBRITIES WHO OWN HOMES IN BRENTWOOD: Anne Archer, Bea Arthur, Antonio Banderas, James Belushi, Peter Bogdanovich, George Carlin, Jim Carrey, Kim Cattrall, Dabney Coleman, Courteney Cox, Cindy Crawford, Robert Culp, Ted Danson, Barbara DeAngelis, Kim Delaney, Phyllis Diller, Blake Edwards and Julie Andrews, Sally Field, Harrison Ford, James Garner, Steve Garvey, Melanie Griffith, Veronica Hamel, Pat Harrington, Tom Hayden, Dustin Hoffman, Janet Jackson, Joanna Kerns, Ron Koslow, Angela Lansbury, George Lazenby, Hal Linden, Zubin Mehta, Kate Mulgrew, Martin Mull, Randy Newman, Julie Newmar, Ken Olin and Patricia Wettig, Michael Ovitz, Rob Reiner, John Ritter, Pat Riley, Mimi Rogers, Roseanne, Rene Russo, Garry Shandling, Patrick Stewart, Rod Stewart, Sally Struthers, Nancy Travis, John Travolta, Robert Wagner and Jill St. John, and Betty White.

Arnold Schwarzenegger and Maria Shriver's Pacific Palisades home.

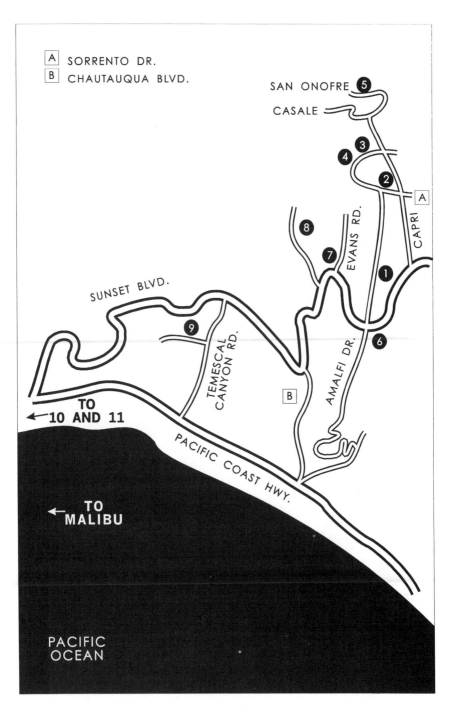

MAP 9 PACIFIC PALISADES

PACIFIC PALISADES

1. THE FIRST HOME OWNED BY RONALD AND NANCY REAGAN IN PACIFIC PALISADES, 1258 Amalfi Drive

The Reagans lived here from 1953 to 1956.

2. FORMER HOME OF SYLVESTER STALLONE, 1570 Amalfi Drive

When Stallone lived here, he constantly fought with his neighbors (including sports broadcaster Vin Scully) over the size of his trees and gates. The house sold in 1989 for $4 million.

3. HOME OWNED BY STEVEN SPIELBERG, 1515 Amalfi Drive

Five-and-a-half foot tall gates block the view of this extraordinary mansion, which was featured in the May 1989 and November 1994 issues of *Architectural Digest*. Spielberg told the magazine: "The history of the house attracted me instinctively. It was important for me to know that David Selznick had lived there during the time he produced *Gone With The Wind*." Other previous owners include Douglas Fairbanks, Jr.; and Cary Grant and Barbara Hutton. Spielberg purchased the mansion in 1985 from singer Bobby Vinton.

4. DAVID NIVEN'S PINK HOUSE, 1461 Amalfi Drive

Niven lived here from 1945 to 1960. In 1994, subsequent owner Whoopi Goldberg married ex-husband Lyle Trachtenberg here. The marriage lasted a year.

5. FORMER RONALD REAGAN HOUSE, 1669 San Onofre Drive

Ronald and Nancy Reagan bought this ranch house in November 1955 and lived here when he was elected president in 1980.

6. "DOOGIE HOWSER, M.D." HOUSE, 796 Amalfi Drive

Producer Steven Bochco used this house in his neighborhood for exterior shots of the Howser residence.

7. EVANS ROAD, Pacific Palisades

Driving on this private road is prohibited by law, and if you get caught trespassing—and are convicted—you could be fined as much as $500 and thrown in jail for a year. Only residents and their guests can drive by the three mansions valued at $8 million, owned by Arnold Schwarzenegger and Maria Shriver. Schwarzenegger originally bought the mansion pictured on page 73 for an estimated $3 million, and then spent another $5 million to buy the homes of his former next-door neighbors, actors John Forsythe and Daniel J. Travanti.

8. WILL ROGERS STATE HISTORIC PARK, 14253 Sunset Boulevard, (310) 454-8212

Situated in this popular public park is the ranch house of humorist and silent screen star Will Rogers, who lived there from 1924 until his death in a plane crash in 1935. After his widow's death in 1944, the grounds were donated to the State of California for use as a public park. The house contains artifacts and memorabilia pertaining to Rogers' career.

In 1984 the park doubled as Golden State Park in San Francisco, where the Klingon ship, commandeered by the "Star Trek" crew, set down in *Star Trek IV: The Voyage Home.* William Shatner uttered one of the more memorable lines of that movie: "Everybody remember where we parked." For house hours and information about the weekend celebrity polo matches, call (310) 454-8212. There is a $5 parking fee.

9. PACIFIC PALISADES HIGH SCHOOL, 15777 Bowdoin Street (west of Temescal Canyon Road and visible from Sunset Boulevard)

This is the high school immortalized by Michael Medved and David Wallechinsky in their bestseller *What Really Happened to the Class of '65?* Their book was a follow-up to a *Time* magazine cover story about American teenagers in the sixties which focused on Pali High's senior class of 1965. Pali alumni include Christie Brinkley, Jeff Bridges, Anthony Edwards, Katey Sagal, Forest Whitaker, Penelope Ann Miller, and the Bangles' Susanna Hoffs. Jennifer Jason Leigh was a Pali dropout.

(DIRECTIONS: To continue the Pacific Palisades tour and head toward Malibu, make a right turn at the intersection of Sunset and Pacific Coast Highway.)

10. SITE OF THELMA TODD'S ROADSIDE CAFE, 17575 Pacific Coast Highway (and 17531 Posetano Road, Todd's apartment above the cafe)

In the 1930s this building housed a popular

celebrity hangout, Thelma Todd's Roadside Cafe, owned by Todd, a popular actress who appeared in 108 films, including *Horsefeathers* with the Marx Brothers. On December 16, 1935, the 29-year-old Todd was found dead in the garage of her apartment above the cafe. She was found slumped behind the wheel of her Lincoln; there was blood on her mink coat and evening dress, the car, the garage floor, and on her head and face. Amazingly, the Los Angeles County coroner ruled her death an accidental suicide, leading to allegations that she may have been murdered, with the murder covered up by the police. Todd's ex-husband was connected with the mob, and rumors persisted that the mob wanted to use the cafe as a gambling den; Todd refused, and was killed for not going along with the plan.

11. J. PAUL GETTY ART MUSEUM, 17985 Pacific Coast Highway, (310) 624-2378

OTHER CELEBRITIES WHO LIVE IN PACIFIC PALISADES: Eddie Albert, Richard Dean Anderson, Dean Cain, Kim Carnes, Tommy Chong, Tom Cruise, Billy Crystal, Dom DeLuise, Harold Gould, Mark Grace, Peter Graves, Steve Guttenberg, Linda Hamilton, Mel Harris, Goldie Hawn, Michael Keaton, Nicole Kidman, Sugar Ray Leonard, Warren Littlefield, Julia Louis-Dreyfuss, Marsha Mason, Walter Matthau, Patrick McGoohan, Ali McGraw, Rita Moreno, Diana Muldaur, Michelle Pfeiffer, Sydney Pollack, Bob Saget, William Schallert, Tracy Ullman, Forest Whitaker, and Brian Wilson.

Thelma Todd's Sidewalk Café, circa 1935.

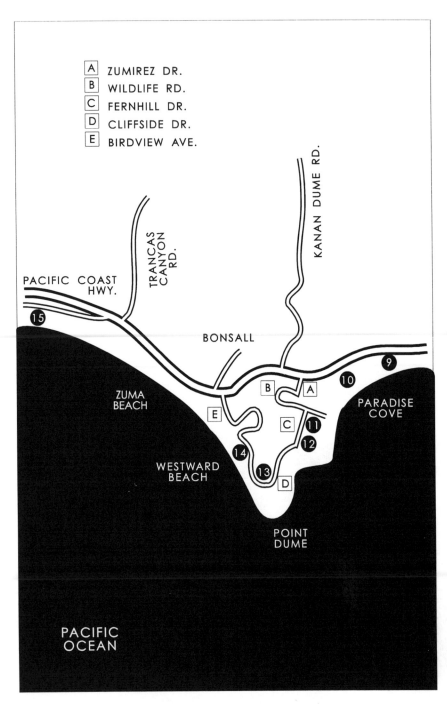

A ZUMIREZ DR.
B WILDLIFE RD.
C FERNHILL DR.
D CLIFFSIDE DR.
E BIRDVIEW AVE.

KANAN DUME RD.

TRANCAS CANYON RD.

PACIFIC COAST HWY.

BONSALL

ZUMA BEACH

PARADISE COVE

WESTWARD BEACH

POINT DUME

PACIFIC OCEAN

MAP 11   MALIBU

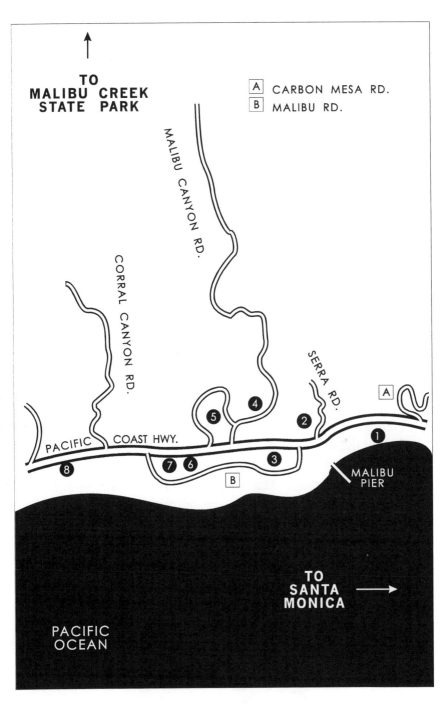

TO
MALIBU CREEK
STATE PARK

A CARBON MESA RD.
B MALIBU RD.

MALIBU CANYON RD.

CORRAL CANYON RD.

SERRA RD.

A

PACIFIC COAST HWY.

5 4 2 1

8 7 6 3

B

MALIBU PIER

TO
SANTA
MONICA

PACIFIC
OCEAN

MAP 10   MALIBU

MALIBU

"Malibu is the only place in the world where you can lie on the sand and look at the stars—or visa versa."

—Joan Rivers

1. CARBON BEACH

Carbon Beach is sometimes referred to as "Deal Beach" since so many entertainment industry executives do business from their summer or weekend beach homes here. "Dealers" include DreamWorks co-founders Jeffrey Katzenberg and David Geffen; and producers Aaron Spelling, Hal Ross, Jerry Bruckheimer, Alan Landsburg and Robert Chartoff.

Carbon Beach also has its fair share of stars. Johnny Carson spent most of the 1980s at 22240 Pacific Coast Highway, which is where he spotted his fourth and most recent wife, Alex Mass, walking along the beach in front of his house. Carson later sold the house to John McEnroe for a reported $1.85 million and six tennis lessons. "Johnny was so serious about the lessons," Carson biographer Laurence Leamer wrote in *King of the Night,* "that the stipulation was included in the sales contract."

In 1991 Janet Jackson bought *Terminator* and *Aliens* producer Gail Ann Hurd's house down the street for $4.5 million.

Bruce Willis and Demi Moore have a home down the street. Others who own homes on the beach: Lloyd Bridges, Brian Wilson, Dani Janssen (David's ex-wife), Flip Wilson, record mogul Irving Azoff, Grammy producer Pierre Cosette, and Jack Klugman

2. SERRA RETREAT

About seven miles north of Carbon Beach is Serra Retreat, a beautiful private community built around a Franciscan spiritual retreat—also called Serra Retreat—nestled in Malibu Canyon. Dick van Dyke, Mel Gibson, Charles Bronson, and George C. Scott live in this community.

The house seen in *The Doctor*, in which the characters played by William Hurt and Christine Lahti lived—and which was supposed to have been in San Francisco—is at 3701 Serra Road.

3. MALIBU COLONY (at 23554 Malibu Road)

Gates and armed security guards keep tourists out of this exclusive and snooty (according to some realtors) celebrity enclave. Colonists include Bruce Dern, Tom Hanks, Norman Jewison, Brian Keith, Burgess Meredith, John McEnroe (who moved here after selling Carson's Carbon Beach home), "Moonlighting" creator Glen Gordon Caron, Rob Reiner, and Sting.

(Note: Malibu Road, just north of the Colony, also attracts many celebrities, most of whom own second homes there. Mel Brooks and Anne Brancroft, Tony Danza, Dom DeLuise, Shirley MacLaine, Charles Bronson, Zubin Mehta, Don Rickles, Loretta Swit and Robert Altman all own houses on Malibu Road.)

A view of the homes in Malibu Colony.

4. HODGES CASTLE, 23800 Malibu Crest Drive

A real castle owned by a dentist. (You will see a few more when you take the Hollywoodland tour.) Patterned after a 13th-Century Scottish castle, the Hodges Castle is perched on a hillside north of Pacific Coast Highway, and can be seen from several directions, including from the gates of Malibu Colony.

5. PEPPERDINE UNIVERSITY, 24255 Pacific Coast Highway

Prestigious, picturesque and private, Pepperdine is a popular filming site. "Battle of the Network Stars" was filmed here.

6. FORMER HOME OF RICH LITTLE, 24734 Pacific Coast Highway

Litttle now resides in Las Vegas.

7. HOME AT 24834 PACIFIC COAST HIGHWAY

In Postcards From the Edge, Meryl Streep shot at Dennis Quaid in this house, where Quaid's character was supposed to have lived.

8. GULLS WAY, 26800 Pacific Coast Highway

Brian Keith, playing Judge Milton C. Hardcastle, lived in this house in the 1983 to 1986 TV series "Hardcastle and McCormick."

9. MALIBU GOLD COAST, 27700 to 27944 Pacific Coast Highway

You will not find the "Malibu Gold Coast" or any points north of Pepperdine on the Auto Club city maps. But if you continue north on Pacific Coast Highway, you will pass a stretch of land that talent agent Charles Stern dubbed "The Malibu Gold Coast"—which describes the beach-front strip of land that runs for a mile or so between his property on private Escondido Beach Road and Paradise Cove to the north. Celebrity residents include America's oldest teenager, Dick Clark (27700 Pacific Coast Highway), and producer Jerry Weintraub, who threw parties for his friend, then-President George Bush, at his home, "Blue Heaven," at 27740 Pacific Coast Highway. Blake Edwards and Julie Andrews lived for years at a home at 27944 Pacific Coast Highway. They sold it in 1992 for a reported $8.5 million. The home has since been torn down so a larger mansion can be built on the site.

10. PARADISE COVE

If you turn left at Paradise Cove Road, and head toward the Sand Castle Restaurant at 28128 Pacific Coast Highway, you will see where a number of popular TV shows and movies have been filmed. James Garner parked his trailer in the parking lot adjacent to the restaurant in "The Rockford Files," and William Conrad's house in "Jake and the Fatman" was the first house on the left of the restaurant.

The Frankie Avalon/Annette Funicello films *Beach Party, Muscle Beach Party, Beach Blanket Bingo* and *Back to the Beach* were all filmed here. In *Indecent Proposal*, Woody Harrelson proposed to Demi Moore on the pier. According to Art Fein's *L.A. Musical History Tour*, "the Beach Boys posed for their first album cover on this stretch of beach."

(Note: The following three houses are located in an area known as Point Dume, south of Pacific Coast Highway.)

11. HOME OF JOHNNY CARSON, 6962 Wildlife Road

Carson purchased this spectacular retreat house, which is situated 200 feet over a cliff, for just under $8.9 million in 1985. According to his biographer Laurence Leamer, Carson also "bought the land across the street, and at a cost of several million dollars constructed one of the most remarkable private tennis court courts in the world. It was not so much a court as a mini-stadium, built recessed so that passers-by could not catch even a glimpse of Johnny playing each day."

12. THE FORMER UNGER ESTATE, 6970 Wildlife Road

In 1985 Madonna and Sean Penn were married at this palatial, $6.5-million clifftop home owned by a friend of the Penn family, Dan Unger, who has been variously identified as a real estate developer and an attorney. In *Madonna Unauthorized*, Christopher Andersen described "the scene at the Unger home more closely resembled a war than a wedding. While armed security guards scanned the horizon with infrared binoculars looking for intruders—namely, members of the press—their blazer-clad brethren checked the credentials of each guest who passed through the ten-foot-high steel gates. Reporters dressed as waiters climbed over the walls, picked up silver trays, and began serving sushi and Cristal champagne to the guests . . . The publicity-loathing Penn, enraged at the presence of the helicopters, ran down to the beach and scrawled FUCK OFF in twenty-foot-high letters in the sand. For nearly a half hour, he paced up and down the beach, shaking his fists at the choppers and yelling profanities. 'He went,' in the words of one guest,

The former Unger Estate (left) and Johnny Carson's home (right).

'completely nuts' . . . and emptied his gun at the helicopter.

13. FORMER HOME OF CHER, 29149 Cliffside Drive
The Academy Award-winning actress and entertainer, who was born Cheryl Sarkisian in 1946, now divides her time between Los Angeles, Manhattan and Aspen, Colorado.

14. WESTWARD BEACH
Music videos filmed here include Madonna's "Cherish" and Vanessa Williams' "Dreamin." At the end of the parking lot is the spot where Charlton Heston finally fled from the apes in *Planet of the Apes*.

15. BROAD BEACH (six miles north of Paradise Cove)
It would probably be fair to say that more celebrities own homes on this mile-and-a-half stretch of land than in any other concentrated living area in the world. Goldie Hawn, Carroll O'Connor, Georgia Rosenbloom, Jack Lemmon, Sylvester Stallone, Jon Bon Jovi, James L. Brooks, Walter Matthau, Grant Tinker, Frank Sinatra, Michael Ovitz, Danny DeVito, Dick Martin, Steve Lawrence and Edie, Dustin Hoffman, Ralph Edwards, Robert Redford, Neil Simon, Walter Hill, Stephanie Beacham, and Eddie van Halen and Valerie Bertenelli, all own weekend or summer houses here. A few celebrities, including director/producer James L. Brooks and Steven Spielberg, own more than one house on the beach. Hugh Hefner, Ted Danson, Chad McQueen, Mel Gibson, Emilio Estevez, Charlie Sheen, and Pat Riley have beach-front houses on the side streets off Broad Beach.

In July 1996, Broad Beach became the site of the infamous "Goldilocks Incident," in which a couple discovered that a strange man had wandered into their house, walked into their son's bedroom, neatly folded his pants over a chair, and gone to sleep in their son's bed. That man was Academy Award-nominated actor, and apparently heroin-addicted, Robert Downey, Jr., who had mistaken their home for a house he was leasing 17 houses away. The incident prompted Jay Leno to joke: "Do you know what the hottest new business on Hollywood Boulevard is? Selling Robert Downey, Jr., a map to his own home."

(Note: Tourists who wish to see celebrity houses up close can do so by walking through a public walkway next to 31346 Broad Beach. The fence is unlocked between sunrise and sunset. There are signs indicating where nonresidents can walk along the shoreline without trespassing.)

Reminder: Do not approach or otherwise disturb the occupants of any of the houses in this book. Stay away from the stars for your own safety!

OTHER CELEBRITIES WHO OWN HOMES IN MALIBU: Pamela Anderson, Pat Benatar, Daniel Benzali, Brian Bosworth, Pierce Brosnan, Cindy Crawford, David Duchovny, Bob Dylan, Joe Eszterhas, Mick Fleetwood, Richard Gere, Henry Gibson, Mark Hamill, Don Henley, John Larroquette, Linda Lavin, Jon Lovitz, Craig T. Nelson, Olivia Newton-John, Nick Nolte, Bronson Pinchot, Rod Steiger, Martin Sheen, Grace Slick, Dean Stockwell, Danny Tartabull and Cindy Williams.

Barbra Streisand, who bought a compound of three homes on Point Dume, donated her previous compound of four homes in Ramirez Canyon to the Santa Monica Mountains Conservancy, which established an environmental think tank, the Streisand Center for Conservancy Studies. The conservancy now offers one-hour guided walking tours of the grounds in which two of Streisand's former houses are shown. The tours cost $30 per person. Reservations are required. For additional information call (310) 589-2850.

Celebrity homes on Malibu's Broad Beach.

Ron Jenny's home on Pacific Coast Highway (not visible from the street) is a favorite of location scouts and has appeared in several movies, most notably *Terminator II,* where it served as the home of actor Joe Morton, who played Miles Dyson, in the movie. The windows you see here are the ones that Linda Hamilton shot out in an attempt to murder Morton and prevent him from inventing the system which results in a nuclear holocaust.

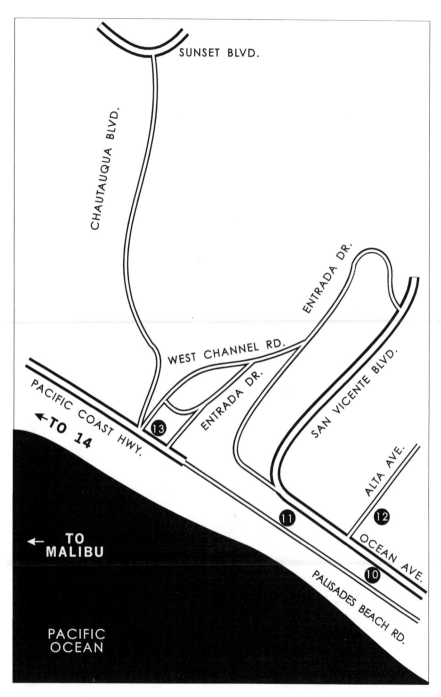

MAP 13   SANTA MONICA

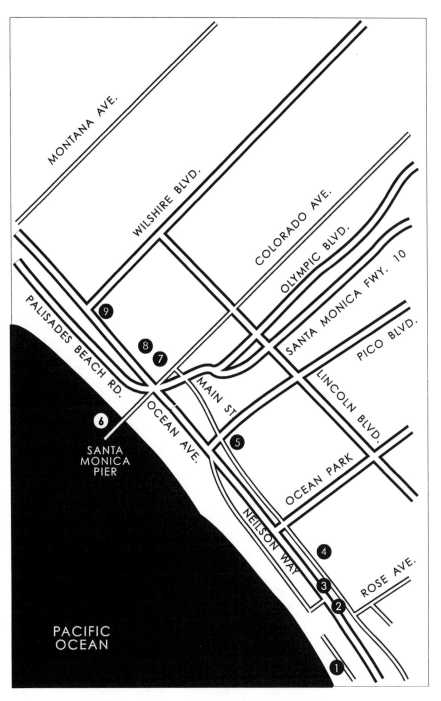

MAP 12 SANTA MONICA

SANTA MONICA
AND VENICE

1. OCEAN FRONT WALK (sometimes referred to as the Venice Boardwalk, Ocean Front Walk extends from Washington Boulevard in Marina del Rey to Marine Street in Santa Monica)

Most of the walk is along Venice Beach, which is famous for its street entertainers, bodybuilders, roller skaters, and the ubiquitous drug pushers, who can often be identified by pagers on their belts. On weekends the atmosphere is carnival-like. The beach here has appeared in countless movies (including *White Men Can't Jump*) and television shows. Fans of "Three's Company," starring John Ritter, Suzanne Somers and Joyce DeWitt, may recall the bicycle scenes at the beach in the opening credits.

2. BALLERINA CLOWN, corner of Rose Avenue and Main Streets

"At the corner of Rose & Main," *Travel and Leisure* magazine notes, "is one of LA's newest landmarks, artist Jonathan Borofsky's monumental sculpture known variously as the Clown, the Dancer or 'that horrid thing.' It's a surreal combination of a clown's head, with a sad Emmett Kelly face, and the body of a tutu-clad ballerina: It's shocking, it's original, it offends the hell out of people. Whatever your opinion, the Ballerina Clown (its real name) serves as a great meeting place, since everyone knows where it is."

3. SCHATZI ON MAIN, 3110 Main Street, (310) 399-4800

Arnold Schwarzenegger frequently dines at this restaurant, which he owns with his wife, Maria Shriver. In fact, Schwarzenegger owns the entire block-long red-brick shopping complex (Main Street Plaza), which consists of three separate buildings. One of the buildings houses his production offices.

The Ballerina Clown in Venice.

4.   STAR WARES ON MAIN, 2817 Main Street (between Ashland and Hill), (310) 399-0224

Star Wares sells clothes that were either once worn by celebrities or worn during concert tours or movie or television performances. Items sold by the store include the rock group KISS's costumes ($33,000 for the entire collection), Madonna's gold cup bustier designed by Jean-Paul Gaultier ($25,000), Michael Jackson's sequined glove ($15,000), Christopher Reeves' *Superman III* costume ($18,000), an extra's costume from *Star Trek: The Next Generation* ($5,000), an arm Arnold Schwarzenegger used in *Terminator II* ($12,000) and a Magic Johnson jersey ($1,000). The store also sells some lower-priced items. Catalogues are available on request. Ten percent of all proceeds go to charity.

5.   SANTA MONICA CIVIC AUDITORIUM, 1855 Main Street (at Pico)

Site of the Academy Awards presentations from 1961 to 1968. The 1996-97 civil trial which found O. J. Simpson responsible for the deaths of his ex-wife Nicole, and Ron Goldman, was held at the county courthouse next door.

6. SANTA MONICA PIER, end of Colorado Avenue (at Ocean Avenue)

Featured in countless television shows and movies, including *Ruthless People;   The Sting; The Net; They Shoot Horses, Don't They?; Clean Slate;* and *Funny Girl.* According to Steven Gaines, author of *Heroes and Villains: The True Story of the Beach Boys,* Brian Wilson once jumped off the pier in a suicide attempt, but was rescued by his brother Dennis.

7. SANTA MONICA PLACE (bounded by 4th and Colorado; 2nd and Broadway)

The mall scenes in *Terminator II* were filmed here, including the fight scenes between the two Terminators, which were filmed in the back hallways, and a scene in which Schwarzenegger was thrown through the window of a clothing store, the Oak Tree. The video arcade was built specially for the movie in an empty storefront. (The producers used the Northridge Mall at 9301 Tampa Avenue, Northridge, for the exterior shots).

Also filmed here was the 1990 feature *Internal Affairs*. A police station was built on the roof of the parking lot. Richard Gere beat up Andy Garcia in an elevator built on the same spot.

The Santa Monica Pier.

8. THIRD STREET PROMENADE (between Broadway and Wilshire Boulevard)

In *A Very Brady Sequel*, the Brady Bunch broke into song outside the Woolworth's at this popular outdoor mall. The promenade features a variety of theaters, bookstores, gift shops, clothing stores and restaurants.

One of the restaurants, the Broadway Café, was also the site of Robert DeNiro's first meeting with Amy Brenneman in *Heat*.

9. LAWRENCE WELK PLAZA, 100 Wilshire Boulevard (at Ocean Avenue)

The 22-story General Telephone Building, now part of the Lawrence Welk Plaza, served as the hospital front for the television series "Marcus Welby, M.D."

10. PETER LAWFORD'S BEACH HOUSE, 625 Palisades Beach Road (which is what Pacific Coast Highway is called beneath Santa Monica's bluffs)

Once film mogul Louis B. Mayer's Santa Monica beach house, this mansion was later owned by actor Peter Lawford and his wife Pat, one of John F. Kennedy's sisters. In *Peter Lawford: The Man Who Kept The Secrets,* author James Spada wrote: "For the first two years of the Kennedy administration, Pat and Peter's beach house was essentially the Western White House. Officially, the President stayed at the Beverly Hilton Hotel, but he spent his days relaxing by his sister and brother-in-law's pool . . . When he was at Peter Lawford's house, he was there to relax and have a good time—and Peter saw to it that he did. Whenever Jack visited when Pat was away, Peter could be counted on to throw a party for him that included, in addition to Peter's show business friends, lovely young starlets, models—and hookers. After an evening of partying, Jack would choose one or two of the prettiest to return with them to his hotel suite. Some of the parties at Lawford's house—those peopled by a great many legendary beautiful women and a great many older married men—became legendary." Lawford's next-door neighbor told author Anthony Summers: "it was nothing but La Dolce Vita over there. It was like a goddamn whorehouse.' And Jack Kennedy hustled his wife. He wanted her to go to Hawaii with him. 'It was the most disgusting thing I've ever seen.'"

11. 415 PCH BEACH CLUB, 415 Palisades Beach Road

This public beach club has an intriguing history. On the site once stood an 118-room, 55-bath mansion that newspaper magnate William Randolph Hearst built in 1928 for his mistress, actress Marion Davies, for a then unheard-of cost of $7 million. Producer Richard Zanuck, who grew up down the street, once remarked: "It made *Gone With the Wind's* Tara look like a guesthouse."

The main house was torn down in 1955, but the servants' wings became part of an exclusive private beach club, the Sand and Sea Club. When the Sand and Sea closed in 1991, the state leased the property for filming— and "Beverly Hills 90210" used the beach club as a focal point for its summer shows.

Now, anyone can park next door, have lunch, and walk, bike or rollerblade on the boardwalk past the club and the beachfront houses of a number of Hollywood legends. These include Harold Lloyd's getaway at 443 Palisades Beach Road, Mae West's at 514, Twentieth-Century Fox head Darryl Zanuck's at 546, Samuel Goldwyn's at 602, Harry Warner's two homes at 605 and 607, Louis B. Mayer and later Peter Lawford's at 625, Douglas Fairbanks and Mary Pickford's at 705, and MGM production chief Irving Thalberg and silent screen star Norma Shearer's at 707.

About a mile down the street, a beach house at 1038 Palisades Beach Road is famous because it was variously lived in by Norma Talmadge; Cary Grant, first with his roommate, Randolph Scott, and then his wife, Barbara Hutton; Princess Grace Kelly; and actress Sharon Tate and her husband, director Roman Polanski.

(A word of caution: Unless you park, you cannot sightsee on Palisades Beach Road—or Pacific Coast Highway—because there is always too much traffic.)

12. FORMER JANE FONDA HOUSE, 316 Alta Drive

Fonda lived here before she married Ted Turner in 1991. The home reportedly sold for close to its $2.7 million asking price.

13. PATRICK'S ROADHOUSE, 106 Entrada Dr. (at Pacific Coast Highway), (310) 459-4544 or 459-6506

Notorious celebrity hangout.

14. LIFEGUARD STATION, TEMESCAL CANYON AND PACIFIC COAST HIGHWAY, around 16000 Pacific Coast Highway

In TV's "Baywatch," David Hasselhoff oversees the lifeguards at this lifeguard station, which is used for both exterior and interior shots. Most of the beach scenes are filmed by the station at Will Rogers State Beach, although the show has also filmed at Santa Monica State Beach, Venice Beach, Paradise Cove, Zuma Beach, and at beaches in Marina del Rey and Long Beach.

NOT ON THE MAP is the new corporate headquarters for MGM Studios at 2500 Broadway Avenue.

Once Hollywood's leading studio, MGM moved from its expansive Culver City lot to this more modest complex of office buildings in 1993. The studio does not offer tours, but tourists can stop in the studio store at 2501 Colorado Avenue to buy T-shirts, coffee mugs, and other goodies with MGM's logo on it. For further information call (800) 405-4646.

Also not on the map is the Venice Pier, located at the end of Washington Boulevard in Venice. The pier was the site of the climactic scene in *Falling Down*, in which Robert Duvall killed Michael Douglas. The pier has been closed for years for repairs, and the filmmakers had to receive special permission to film the scene.

CELEBRITIES WHO LIVE IN SANTA MONICA: Debbie Allen, Jason Bateman, Mel Brooks and Anne Bancroft, Jackson Browne, Suzi Chaffee, David Clennon, Roger Corman, Wes Craven, Michael Crichton, Blythe Danner, Dana Delaney, Joyce DeWitt, Richard Dysart, Lou Ferrigno, Paul Michael Glaser, Tony Goldwin, Shelley Hack, Barbara Hershey, Dwayne Hickman, Susanna Hoffs, Christine Lahti, June Lockhart, Julianna Margulies, Kevin McCarthy, Penelope Anne Miller, Tracy Nelson, Randy Newman, Paula Poundstone, Harold Ramis, Helen Reddy, Joe Regalbuto, Ving Rhames, Sugar Ray Robinson, Suzanne Somers, Oliver Stone, Wendy Wilson and Robin Wright.

Matt Groening, Dennis Hopper, and Ed O'Neill live near the beach in Venice. Florence Henderson lives on a yacht in Marina del Rey.

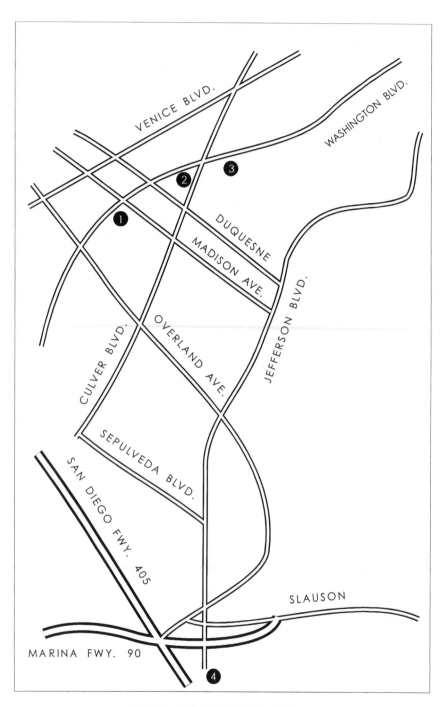

MAP 14 CULVER CITY

CULVER CITY

1. SONY ENTERTAINMENT, 10202 W. Washington Boulevard

Located on the former MGM lot, Sony is the parent company of Columbia Pictures and Tri-Star Pictures, entertainment companies which film many of their features on the sound stages here. The studio does not offer a tour.

2. OLD CULVER CITY HOTEL, 9400 Culver Boulevard

In 1938 most of the Munchkins stayed in this triangular-shaped hotel during the filming of *The Wizard of Oz*.

3. THE CULVER STUDIOS, 9336 Washington Boulevard

Owned by Sony Pictures Entertainment and often rented out to other studios, the Culver Studios is the most interesting studio in Culver City to drive by. The main attraction is the neo-colonial white mansion seen in the opening credits of all the David O. Selznick movies, including *Gone With the Wind*. The burning of Atlanta and other scenes from the movie were filmed on the back lot along Ballona Creek, but the site is now an industrial tract. Selznick, who also produced *Rebecca, King Kong*, and the original *A Star is Born*, was one of many to own the studio. Others include movie pioneer Thomas Ince, Cecil B. DeMille, RKO-Pathe, Howard Hughes, Desilu, Laird International Studios and Grant Tinker. Interior shots for *E.T., City Slickers, A Few Good Men,* and *Ghosts of Mississippi* were filmed here. Visitors are not allowed.

4. HILLSIDE CEMETERY, 6001 Centinela Avenue

When you drive on the San Diego Freeway (the 405), between the airport and the West L.A., you cannot miss the six-column marble shrine to Al Jolson, who appeared in *The Jazz Singer,* the first motion picture with synchronized sound. The memorial depicts him down on one knee, singing with his arms outstretched. Jack Benny and Mary Livingstone Benny, Eddie Cantor, Percy Faith, David Janssen, George A. Jessel, Vic Morrow, Jerry Rubin, and Allan Sherman are also entombed at Hillside.

(Holy Cross Cemetery, located at 5835 W. Slauson Avenue, is located nearby. Ray Bolger, John Candy, Bing Crosby, Jimmy Durante, Spike Jones, Mario Lanza, Bela Lugosi, Louella Parsons, and Sharon Tate are buried there.)

WESTWOOD AND CENTURY CITY

1. DEAD MAN'S CURVE, Sunset Boulevard (across from the UCLA football field)

Many people believed that "Dead Man's Curve," immortalized in song by Jan and Dean, referred to one of the curves on Mulholland Drive. Others believed it referred to a curve on Whittier Boulevard, by Buddy Hackett's house, where Jan Berry, one of the songwriters, was involved in a near-fatal car crash. (That accident actually happened after the song was released.) In *The L.A. Musical History Tour,* Art Fein reports that both Jan and Dean and co-writer Roger Christian agree "Dead Man's Curve" referred to a particularly curvy stretch of Sunset Boulevard across from the UCLA football field. Though most of Sunset Boulevard around UCLA and Beverly Hills remains curvy, Dead Man's Curve no longer exists. According to Fein, it was regraded after comedian Mel Blanc suffered a near-fatal crash there. (Note: The chase scenes from *Against All Odds* were filmed on Sunset between Veteran Avenue and Beverly Glen Boulevard.)

2. UCLA, 405 Hilgard Avenue

UCLA boasts one of the finest film schools in the country. UCLA alumni in the arts include Jim Morrison, who, contrary to the impression left in Oliver Stone's *The Doors,* was actually graduated with honors; Francis Ford Coppola, screenwriter Shane Black; Carol Burnett; Mark

107

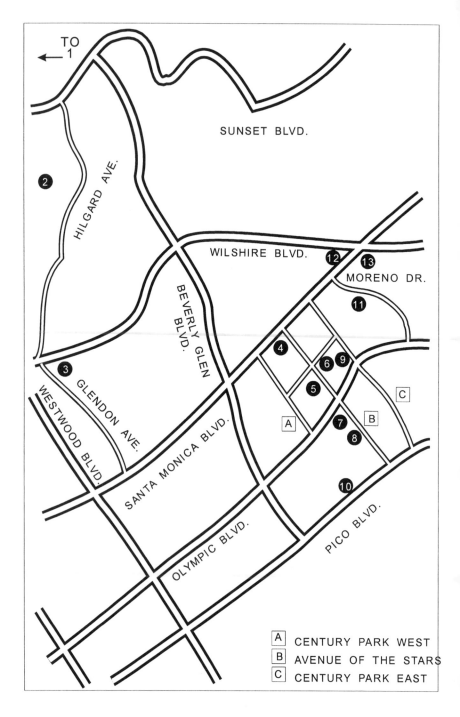

MAP 15. WESTWOOD & CENTURY CITY

Harmon; Kareem Abdul-Jabbar; Tim Robbins; Marilyn McCoo; Michael Ovitz; conductor John Williams; Daphne Zuniga; and James Dean. Heather Locklear and director-actor Rob Reiner are two one of UCLA's more famous dropouts.

UCLA is also a frequent location site. The 1996 remake of *The Nutty Professor*, starring Eddie Murphy, and the 1985 feature *Gotcha!*, starring Anthony Edwards, were filmed extensively on campus. So were many scenes from Reiner's *The Sure Thing*. UCLA has also appeared in *Threesome, The Big Fix, Final Analysis, Mr. Baseball*, and hundreds of commercials and television shows.

3. WESTWOOD VILLAGE MEMORIAL PARK AND MORTUARY, 1218 Glendon Avenue

The cemetery, which is a little difficult to find (the driveway entrance is tucked away between an office building at the southeast corner of Wilshire Boulevard and a parking structure), attracts tourists who wish to pay their respects to Marilyn Monroe. Someday Marilyn will be kept company by Hugh Hefner, who bought the crypt adjacent to hers. Hefner paid an estimated $25,000 for the privilege of spending eternity next to the woman who launched his *Playboy* empire.

Near Marilyn's crypt, which is located in the Corridors of Memories, are the graves of two of the children from the *Poltergeist* movies (Dominique Dunne, who was strangled by her boyfriend; and Heather "They're here" O'Rourke, who died of a rare intestinal deformity at the age of 12); Dean Martin; 1980 *Playboy* Playmate of the Year Dorothy Stratten, whose story was memorialized in the chilling *Star 80* starring Eric Roberts and Mariel Hemingway; Twentieth-Century Fox production chief Darryl F. Zanuck; historians Will and Ariel Durant;

Natalie Wood; Donna Reed; Truman Capote; Buddy Rich; and Roy Orbison.

Peter Lawford was buried here, but his last wife Patty removed Lawford's ashes when cemetary officials insisted Lawford's crypt be fully paid for. According to James Spada, author of *Peter Lawford: The Man Who Kept the Secrets,* when Lawford was evicted from the cemetery, Patty made a deal with the *National Enquirer* "giving the tabloid exclusive picture rights in exchange for the limousine to take her to Marina del Rey, and a boat which to scatter Peter's ashes in the Pacific . . . Newspapers around the country told the story of Peter Lawford's last great indignity—his eviction from his final resting place."

4. CENTURY CITY SHOPPING CENTER & MAR-KETPLACE, 10250 Santa Monica Boulevard, (310) 277-3898

Offers free parking for three hours. More and more movie premieres are held at the theaters here.

5. CENTURY PLAZA HOTEL AND TOWER, 2025 Avenue of the Stars

One of Los Angeles' premier hotels, the Century Plaza is a frequent site of celebrity fundraisers. In 1972 Marilyn McCoo and Billy Davis, Jr., of the Fifth Dimension, were married behind the hotel and flew up, up and away in a hot air balloon.

6. ABC ENTERTAINMENT CENTER, 2020 and 2040 Avenue of the Stars

The complex includes the Shubert Theater, movie theaters, offices, and restaurants.

7. FOX PLAZA, 2121 Avenue of the Stars

Located just yards from the back gate of 20th Century Fox, this is the building used as the site of the Nakatomi Corporation in *Die Hard.* Bruce Willis tried to rescue hostages taken in the 33rd and 34th floors of the building, which was chosen for its high-tech look. Ironically, the building, owned by Fox at the time of the filming, was later sold to a Japanese concern. Ronald Reagan had his postpresidential offices here. The building was also depicted as the site of Anthony LaPlagia's law firm in the ABC drama "Murder One."

8. PARK HYATT LOS ANGELES, 2151 Avenue of the Stars (at Galaxy Way), (310) 277-2777; (800) 233-1234

In *Lethal Weapon 2* Mel Gibson and Danny Glover guarded Joe Pesci in the presidential suite of the Park Hyatt, and their stuntmen jumped into the swimming pool. (The hotel was also used for the pool jump scene in *Harley Davidson and the Marlboro Man.)* Also filmed here were the scenes in *Pacific Heights* in which Melanie Griffith, investigating Michael Keaton, tracked him to a room at the hotel. In *Point of No Return*, Bridget Fonda planted a bomb, which destroyed part of the hotel.

9. CENTURY PLAZA TOWERS, 2029 and 2049 Century Park East

These twin office towers were supposed to be the location of Cybill Shepherd and Bruce Willis' Blue Moon Detective Agency in "Moonlighting," and Stephanie Zimbalist and Pierce Brosnan's Steele Investigations in "Remington Steele."

A view of Century City, including the Century Plaza Towers (center), Fox Plaza, where *Die Hard* was filmed (right), and 20th Century Fox (bottom right).

10. TWENTIETH CENTURY FOX, 10201 W. Pico Boulevard

Unfortunately, Fox does not offer public tours, and virtually the only way to catch a glimpse of its back lot is to get tickets for one of the shows filming on the lot from one of the audience service companies. From the main entrance on Pico Boulevard, you can see part of the set built for *Hello Dolly!* in the late 1960s. The studio has been located here since 1930.

11. BEVERLY HILLS HIGH SCHOOL, 241 S. Moreno Drive, Beverly Hills

Tourists sometimes drive past Beverly Hills High School thinking they will see the fictional West Beverly High in the television series "Beverly Hills 90210." Actually, the producers used Torrance High School in the Los Angeles suburb of Torrance, where filming permit costs are about one-fourth of what the city of Beverly Hills charges. Beverly Hills High School is still of interest, though, since it is one of the best high schools in the country. Its celebrity graduates include Desi Arnaz, Jr., Corbin Bernsen, Albert Brooks, Nicolas Cage, Shaun and Patrick Cassidy, Richard Chamberlain, Jamie Lee Curtis, Barry Diller, Richard Dreyfuss, Nora Ephron, Carrie Fisher, Rhonda Fleming, Bonnie Franklin, Joel Grey, Crispin Glover, Julie Kavner, Lenny Kravitz, Penny Marshall, Laraine Newman, Rain Pryor, Rob Reiner, David Schwimmer, Pauly Shore, Jonathan Silverman, Marlo Thomas, Burt Ward, and Betty White.

It's a Wonderful Life was filmed on campus and there is a scene in the movie in which Jimmy Stewart and Donna Reed fell into the swimming pool there. The school was also lampooned in the feature film, *The Beverly Hillbillies*.

12.   BEVERLY HILTON HOTEL, 9876 Wilshire Boulevard, (310) 274-7777

The first Grammy Awards ceremonies were held at this hotel.   In recent years the hotel has hosted the Golden Globe Awards and numerous celebrity fundraisers.

Richard Nixon made his famous "you-won't-have-Nixon-to-kick around-anymore" speech here after losing the 1962 California gubernatorial election.

13.   HEADQUARTERS OF CREATIVE ARTISTS AGENCY (CAA), 9830 Wilshire Boulevard (at Little Santa Monica Boulevard)

Creative Artists Agency is generally regarded to be the most powerful talent-management agency in Hollywood.   Its three-story headquarters was designed by the internationally renowned architect I. M. Pei.

Directly across the street, at 9882 Little Santa Monica Boulevard, is the Peninsula Beverly Hills Hotel, one of the highest-rated hotels in the city.   Many CAA clients dine or stay at the hotel, making it one of the best places for celebrity-watching.

CELEBRITIES WHO OWN HOMES IN WESTWOOD: Carol Burnett, Placido Domingo, Charles Durning, Jim Nabors, and Tori Spelling all live in high-rises on Wilshire Boulevard. Ray Bradbury, Jamie Lee Curtis, Michele Lee, John Lithgrow, Laraine Newman, Michelle Phillips, and Mark Spitz live nearby in West Los Angeles.

"Hard Copy," quoting pop star Michael Jackson's former maid, identified the Westford condominium at 10750 Wilshire Boulevard as "The Hideaway" where Jackson allegedly took his "special friends."

Down the street, just west of the intersection of Wilshire Boulevard and Selby Avenue, is the site where 1960s yippie-turned-yuppie Jerry Rubin was struck by a car while jaywalking across Wilshire Boulevard. Rubin later died of internal injuries at UCLA Medical Center.

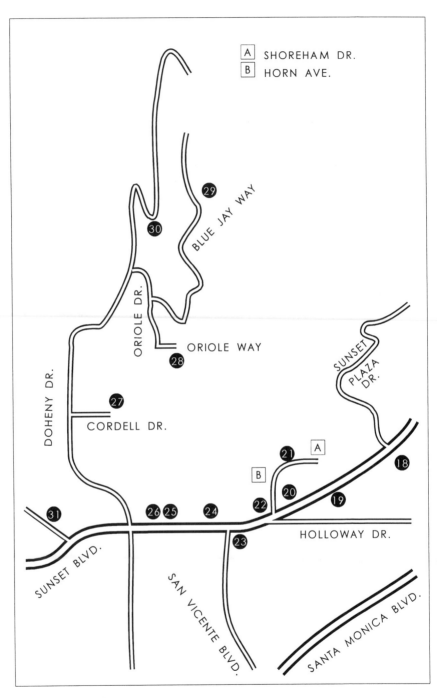

MAP 17 THE SUNSET STRIP

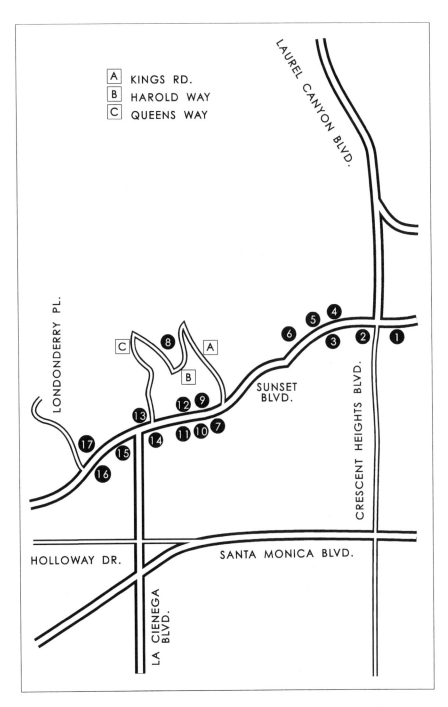

MAP 16 THE SUNSET STRIP

THE SUNSET STRIP

NOTE TO READERS: This is mostly a walking tour of what is often called Hollywood's playground: the Sunset Strip. This tour also includes a few homes in the hills north of the Strip which are best reachable by car. Most of the sites in this tour are within the city limits of West Hollywood (the dividing line between Los Angeles and West Hollywood is Sunset Boulevard; anything north of the Boulevard or east of the Chateau Marmont is within Los Angeles city limits). Sites south of Sunset Boulevard are included in the West Hollywood section. Those who walk the Strip should keep in mind that a few sites listed in the West Hollywood section, including the apartment where Sal Mineo was stabbed to death, and the apartment where Judith Campbell Exner lived when she had her affair with JFK, are within one or two blocks of Sunset Boulevard.

1. FORMER SITE OF SCHWAB'S PHARMACY, 8024 Sunset Boulevard (southeast corner of Crescent Heights)

Schwab's was the most famous drugstore in America, partly because its owner, pharmacist Leon Schwab, kept claiming that Lana Turner was "discovered" sitting on a stool at the soda fountain in his store. Turner herself has said on several occasions that there is no truth to the story, and it appears the tale was concocted by Schwab to lure customers to the store.

There is, at least, truth to the story that in its heyday Schwab's was a popular hangout for writers and actors looking for work. In the movie *Sunset Boulevard*, William Holden called it "a combination office, coffee klatch and waiting room." Schwab filled prescriptions for studio executives and claimed he told them about some of the young budding actors who he thought were star material.

While Lana Turner was not discovered there, one regular, author F. Scott Fitzgerald, did have a heart attack there while buying cigarettes. The pharmacy was torn down in 1988 to make room for a block-long shopping complex now anchored by Virgin Records.

2. FORMER SITE OF THE GARDEN OF ALLAH, 8152 Sunset Boulevard

Remember the song "Big Yellow Taxi," in which Joni Mitchell sang about paving paradise and putting up a parking lot? That was a reference to the tearing down of the Garden of Allah, another famous Hollywood landmark which once stood on the southwest corner of Sunset and Crescent Heights, directly across the street from Schwab's. The apartment/hotel was what one writer called the unofficial epicenter of Hollywood social activity during the 1930s and 1940s, with Frank Sinatra, Ava Gardner, Clark Gable, David Niven, Errol Flynn, the Marx Brothers, Robert Benchley, F. Scott Fitzgerald, Tallulah Bankhead, Clara Bow, Humphrey Bogart, Ernest Hemingway, and Leopold Stokowski among the major celebrities who were Garden residents at one time or another.

According to Bruce Torrence, author of *Hollywood: The First 100 Years:* "It was not uncommon to see tourists and movie fans lining the sidewalk just to get a glimpse of their favorite star." Torrence called the

Garden's inhabitants "a fast-living, hard-drinking, high-rolling lot who burned out fast and took the Garden with them." In 1950 the Garden was sold to Lytton Savings and Loan, which tore it down and built its home office at the site. The site is now a minimall and a branch of Great Western Bank.

3. "ROCKY AND BULLWINKLE" STATUE, 8218 Sunset Boulevard

This converted house, once owned by Fess Parker, TV's "Davy Crockett," was for years the offices of Jay Ward Productions, the animation company that created "Rocky and Bullwinkle." A 15-foot-tall plaster statue of the famous moose and squirrel still stands in front of the building, as does a small courtyard which bears signatures of June Foray (the voices of both Rocky and Natasha) and, strangely enough, the elbowprints of the cartoon's writers. Rocky and Bullwinkle saluted a once-existing billboard for a Las Vegas hotel in the 1960s, which featured a showgirl in a bathing suit. Whenever the showgirl got a new bathing suit, Bullwinkle got a new one with colors to match.

4. CHATEAU MARMONT, 8221 Sunset Boulevard, (213) 656-1010

When celebrities visiting Los Angeles want to be seen, they often go to the Beverly Hills Hotel. When they wish to keep out of the limelight they often stay at the Marmont. In his book *Life at the Marmont*, co-authored with Fred E. Basten, former owner Raymond L. Sarlot noted that the Marmont remains "one of [Hollywood's] best kept secrets, much to the joy of its celebrated clientele. Not too many years ago a *Newsday* journalist cornered Jill Clayburgh sipping coffee at [the hotel's

The coroner's van and the media circus outside the Chateau Marmont on the day John Belushi died of a drug overdose.

coffee shop]. Following the usual career questions, she was asked to comment about her stay at the Marmont. 'Oh, don't mention the hotel,' she said, crinkling her face. 'Then all the tourists will come.' A moment later, Clayburgh was on her way, but not before leaving the journalist with a final thought. 'If you must say something about this place, say it's terrible. Please say it's terrible.'

The fact that tourists have not discovered the hotel yet is one of the reasons why stars like Marilyn Monroe, Warren Beatty, Dustin Hoffman, John Lennon and Yoko Ono, Ringo Starr, Bob Dylan, Mick Jagger, Jim Morrison, Roman Polanski, Greta Garbo, Keanu Reeves, and Sarah Jessica Parker have all stayed for extended periods. One former guest, John Belushi, did attract crowds when he died of a drug overdose on March 4, 1982, in bungalow 3. In the movie *The Doors* Val Kilmer, playing Jim Morrison, was seen trying to leap out of a sixth-floor penthouse.

5. CAJUN BISTRO, 8301 Sunset Boulevard (at Sweetzer), (213) 656-6388

This restaurant was formerly the Source, the natural foods restaurant where Diane Keaton dumped Woody Allen in *Annie Hall.*

6. MANSION OWNED BY JOHNNY DEPP (high on the hillside just west of Sweetzer Avenue)

When actor Johnny Depp bought this 29-room mansion in 1995, some entertainment magazines reported that it was once owned by Bela Lugosi and that the Munchkins stayed there during the filming of *The Filming of Oz.* Hollywood historian Laurie Jacobson insists that neither claim is correct, and that the castle only *looks* like the type of home the one-time *Dracula* star might have lived in.

In fact, the castle was once owned by Hersee Moody Carson, the childless widow of a multimillionaire, and it was called the "Castle of the Fairy Lady" because she used to hold parties there for orphans on major holidays during the 1930s and 1940s. Before Depp shelled out $2.3 million for the gated estate, it was owned by divorce attorney Michael Mitchelson, who lost it in a bankruptcy after being convicted of tax fraud.

What you can see from Sunset, behind thick foliage, is the backside of the mansion. The front entrance is on North Sweetzer Avenue.

7. THE ARGYLE, 8358 Sunset Boulevard, (213) 654-7100

This luxury hotel was once the Sunset Towers, the home to Hollywood stars such as John Wayne, Marilyn Monroe, Clark Gable, Errol Flynn, Howard Hughes, Roger Moore, and the Gabor sisters. One resident, Bugsy Siegel, was reportedly asked to leave after he was arrested for placing bets at the hotel.

The building itself is an intriguing 13-story Art Deco tower emblazoned with mythological creatures, zeppelins, airplanes, and Adam and Eve.

The club is occasionally used as a film location and has served as the outside of the Voltaire Restaurant in *Pretty Woman*, John Travolta's hotel room in *Get Shorty*, actor Stuart Margolin's apartment in *Guilty by Suspicion,* and Richard Crenna's apartment in the short-lived TV series "Pros and Cons." Tim Robbins was pitched a story idea at the Argyle poolside in *The Player*.

8. LIBERACE HOME, 8433 Harold Way (between Kings and Queens Road)

Liberace lived in this 28-room mansion from 1961 to 1979. He told his biographer Bob Thomas, author of *Liberace*: "I tried to turn this place into a museum. In one month we had seventeen thousand reservations. But the neighbors complained" about traffic from the tourists. Liberace's museum was instead built in Las Vegas.

The Argyle Hotel.

9. HYATT ON SUNSET, 8401 Sunset Boulevard (at Kings Road), (213) 656-4101

In the 1960s and 1970s, when the hotel was the Continental Hyatt House, and a favorite of rock and rollers, the hotel was better known as "The Riot House." According to Art Fein's *L.A. Musical History Tour* book, "Led Zeppelin rented as many as six floors here for their carryings on. Their partying set a standard that has never been equaled, with orgies, motorcycles in the halls, and stories yet untold." Fein also reports that "The Rolling Stones movie *Cocksucker Blues* shows Keith Richards and Bobby Keyes throwing a television out a window of this hotel" and that the Doors' "Jim Morrison lived here until he was evicted by management for hanging out a window by his fingertips, dangling over the pavement." Little Richard lived here through much of the 1980s and 1990s.

11. HOUSE OF BLUES, 8430 Sunset Boulevard (at Olive), (213) 848-5100

Investors in this nightclub include Blues Brother Dan Aykroyd.

12. COMEDY STORE, 8433 Sunset Boulevard, (213) 656-6225

One of Los Angeles' premier comedy clubs, the Comedy Store has featured performances from every important comedian. The names of its headliners are vaunted on its outside walls. This was once the site of Ciro's, one of Hollywood's most popular nightclubs during the 1940s and 1950s.

13. PIAZZA DEL SOL, 8439 Sunset Boulevard

This Spanish Revival apartment building was designated a historic landmark because of its beauty, not because of its notorious history. During the 1930s, this was the site of Lee Francis' "House of Francis," the classiest brothel on the Sunset Strip. The building now houses the offices of several production companies—the names of which most people would not recognize—and the brothels are now located in private homes above the Strip.

14. MONDRIAN HOTEL, 8440 Sunset Boulevard (at Queens Road), (213) 650-8999

This classy hotel caters to celebrities in the music, entertainment, and fashion industries. Members of Guns and Roses, The Who, Hole (including Courtney Love), the Smashing Pumpkins, the Cranberries, Public Enemy, Gipsy Kings, and Poison have stayed here, as have many actors. In the movie *Doc Hollywood*, Michael J. Fox stayed in room 1110. The hotel's nightclub, "Sky Bar," which provides panoramic views of the city, is so popular that hotel employees refer to it as "celebrity central."

15. SITE OF "77 SUNSET STRIP," 8532 Sunset Boulevard

Although fans of the popular 1950s TV series would never recognize it today, the front door of the Tiffany Theater is where Efrem Zimbalist, Jr., and Roger Smith played private eyes at the fictitious address "77 Sunset Strip." The restaurant next to their offices, Dino's Lodge—which was once owned by Dean Martin—is also gone. It has been replaced by an office building housing Casablanca Records. Fans of the show will remember Edd "Kookie" Byrnes parking cars at Dino's Lodge.

16. PLAYBOY STUDIO WEST, 8560 Sunset Boulevard

Location of Playboy Studio West, where many of Playboy's famous centerfolds and photo layouts are shot. Sorry, guys, no tours.

17. APARTMENT AT 1326 LONDONDERRY VIEW (one block north of Sunset, off Londonderry Place)

Jane Wyman lived in apartment 5 here in the late 1930s, just three blocks from Ronald Reagan's house at 1128 Cory Avenue. After they married on January 26, 1940, Reagan moved in with her. However, the apartment proved to be too small after their first daughter, Maureen, was born, and the Reagans built a house at nearby 9137 Cordell Drive (covered later on the tour, page 129).

18. SUNSET PLAZA

This is a two-block cluster of hip outdoor cafes, boutiques, hair salons, and other stores whose prices rival those of Rodeo Drive's. It is one of the best people-watching places in town.

(NOTE: Tourists often ask how to get to the top of the mountain above the Sunset Strip to get some of the most commanding views of the Strip and the city below. It is possible to get there by taking a side trip up Sunset Plaza Drive. Just follow it continuously for about fifteen minutes, as Sunset Plaza Drive becomes Appian Way at the crest of the mountain. Then make a right onto Stanley Hills, and another right on Lookout Mountain, which dead-ends at Laurel Canyon Boulevard. Turn right on Laurel Canyon if you want to return to the Strip. This is not my favorite tour through the Hollywood Hills—the homes are not as unique or as impressive as they are elsewhere in the Hills—but the trip is worth trying once.)

19. LE DOME RESTAURANT, 8720 Sunset Boulevard, (310) 659-6919

People magazine calls "the mammoth circular bar at Le Dome is one of L.A.'s best meet-and-mate spots. Here Sylvester Stallone often wooed Brigitte Nielsen, Rod Stewart met Rachel Hunter and Don Johnson and Melanie Griffith rekindled romance." Author Jackie Collins calls Le Dome "definitely THE place to have that power lunch."

20. SPAGO, 1114 Horn Avenue, (310) 652-4025

The most famous restaurant in Los Angeles and the place where the biggest stars party on Academy Awards Night.

21. SHOREHAM TOWERS, 8787 Shoreham Drive (at Horn)

David Lee Roth and Neil Sedaka are among the celebrity residents of this condominium complex. A house that Humphrey Bogart shared with his Mayo Method, his second wife, once stood on this site.

Art Linkletter's daughter Diane, after taking LSD, jumped to her death from a sixth-floor apartment here in 1969. Ballet star turned actor Alexander Godunov died in his condo here of alcohol abuse in 1995.

22. TOWER RECORDS, 8801 Sunset Boulevard, (310) 657-7300

The store, which is often featured in national news stories about the record business, was held up by Jane Fonda and George Segal in the feature film *Fun With Dick and Jane.*

23. THE VIPER ROOM, 8852 Sunset Boulevard

On October 31, 1993, 23-year-old River Phoenix died of a drug overdose outside this nightclub owned by Johnny Depp. Depp told an interviewer he named the club "after a group of musicians who called themselves Vipers. They were reefer heads and they helped start modern music." In the 1940s, the club was known as the Melody Room and was a notorious hangout for Los Angeles mobsters.

24. THE WHISKY, 8901 Sunset Boulevard (at Clark Street)

This was the West Coast's first discotheque. "Gogo" dancing was born here.

25. THE ROXY, 9009 Sunset Boulevard, (310) 276-2222

The Roxy is one of Los Angeles' top music clubs and showcases for new talent. Although nearby restaurants claim otherwise, John Belushi had his last supper here at On The Rox, an exclusive private club above the Roxy.

26. RAINBOW BAR AND GRILL, 9015 Sunset Boulevard, (310) 278-4232

Vincente Minnelli proposed to Judy Garland, and Marilyn Monroe met her future husband, Joe DiMaggio, on a blind date, when the Grill's predecessor, the Villa Nova Restaurant, was here.

27. HOUSE AT 9137 CORDELL DRIVE (north of Doheny Drive)

Ronald Reagan lived here with his first wife, Jane Wyman, from 1941 until their divorce in 1948. According to Anne Edwards' biography *Early Reagan*, he separated from Wyman several times during 1947 and 1948, and during two of those separations he moved into the Garden of Allah. After the house was sold, Reagan moved back to an apartment at 1326 Londonderry View. (After marrying Nancy Davis in 1952, Reagan moved into Nancy's apartment in Brentwood, and then they bought a house in Pacific Palisades.)

28. FORMER MADONNA HOME, 9045 Oriole Way

Madonna bought this gated three-bedroom house for $3 million in 1989 from Allen Questron, the former president and CEO of Neiman Marcus, and sold it for $2 million during California's 1994 real estate slump.

29. BLUE JAY WAY (side street off Oriole Drive)

In his book *L.A. Musical History Tour*, Art Fein reports that "George Harrison rented a house on this street in 1968, just before the Beatles recorded Magical Mystery Tour. Their publicist Derek Taylor had such difficulty finding the place in the fog one night that Harrison penned 'Blue Jay Way,' a dreamy paean to it, which emerged on that album. The street might still be hard to find, because residents report that the street sign is frequently stolen by Beatle(klepto)-maniacs."

30. HOUSE AT 1654 DOHENY DRIVE

This three-story Spanish house is famous for two reasons. According to her memoir *Madame 90210*, Hollywood madam Alex Adams operated a brothel here for several years before her 1988 arrest. The house was subsequently rented by actress Shannen Doherty during the years she starred on "Beverly Hills 90210." According to a lawsuit filed by her former landlord, Doherty trashed the home and left in the dead of night owing $14,000 in overdue rent.

31. SIERRA TOWERS, 9255 Doheny Drive

Jack Webb lived and died in this exclusive high-rise condominium complex. Actor Peter Lawford also lived here in the late 1960s and early 1970s, after he sold his beach house in Santa Monica. Lawford moved out of Sierra Towers after the 6.4 earthquake that shook Los Angeles on February 9, 1971, reportedly because he did not like the way the building swayed in the quake.

(NOTE: Tourists who wish to combine the Sunset Strip and Beverly Hills tours can do so by continuing west on Doheny. Hillcrest Drive—which is where the Beverly Hills tour in this book starts—is just two blocks west of Sierra Towers on Doheny. See page 19.)

CELEBRITIES WHO OWN HOMES IN THE HOLLYWOOD HILLS ABOVE THE SUNSET STRIP: Bess Armstrong, Halle Berry, Jim Brown, Richard Donner, Robert Downey Jr., James Farentino, Larry Flynt, Robin Givens, Herbie Hancock, Katherine Helmond, Buck Henry, Sherman Hemsley, Tom Hulce, Jackee, Richard Lewis, Jon Lovitz, Dinah Manoff, Ed Marinaro, Johnny Mathis, Marlee Matlin, Ricardo Montalban, Judd Nelson, Leslie Nielsen, Donna Pescow, Lionel Ritchie, Jerry Seinfeld, Richard Simmons, Cheryl Tiegs, and "Weird Al" Yankovic.

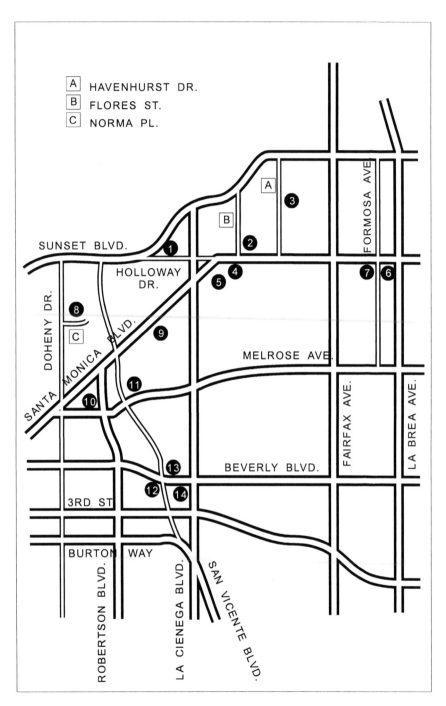

MAP 18 WEST HOLLYWOOD

WEST HOLLYWOOD

1. SITE OF SAL MINEO STABBING, 8563 Holloway Drive (one block south of Sunset Boulevard, between Alta Loma Road and Westmount Drive)

The 37-year-old actor, who is best known for his Academy Award-nominated performance in *Rebel Without a Cause,* was stabbed to death on February 12, 1976, in the carport of this apartment building owned by attorney Marvin Mitchelson. Mineo lived next door at 8565 Holloway Drive. Next door to that apartment, at 8573 Holloway, is another apartment that Marilyn Monroe shared with Shelley Winters in 1951.

2. FORMER APARTMENT OF JFK MISTRESS JUDITH CAMPBELL EXNER, 1200 N. Flores Street

Exner is the woman who had simultaneous affairs with President John F. Kennedy and mobster Sam Giancana during Kennedy's White House years. She also claims to have served as a courier between the two, carrying envelopes back and forth between them in 1960 and 1961. (Although she claims she never peeked inside, she believes the envelopes carried payoffs intended to influence the 1960 presidential election.) Frank Sinatra reportedly introduced Exner to JFK. In 1961 Exner lived here, in apartment 201. In her autobiography *My Story,* she claimed she was harassed by FBI agents who learned of her affair with Kennedy, and in 1962 moved to another apartment at nearby 8401 Fountain Avenue.

3. COLONIAL HOUSE, 1416 N. Havenhurst Drive

Julia Roberts, Bette Davis, Clark Gable, Carole Lombard and her husband Dick Powell all lived in this French colonial apartment building. So did Sammy Glick, the protagonist in Budd Schulberg's classic novel of Hollywood, *"What Makes Sammy Run?"*

4. EMSER RUGS AND TILE, 8431 Santa Monica Boulevard (one block east of La Cienega Boulevard)

In the first *Lethal Weapon*, a suicidal Mel Gibson tried to talk a suicidal man out of jumping off the building. Gibson went nuts and they both ended up taking a plunge off the building into an air bag.

5. BARNEY'S BEANERY, 8447 Santa Monica Boulevard, (213) 654-2287

This old-time diner was once frequented by musicians like Janis Joplin and Jim Morrison. It is still considered a rock 'n rollers' hangout. Actors-turned-directors Penny Marshall and Rob Reiner met here in 1969. They are now divorced.

6. WARNER HOLLYWOOD STUDIOS, 1041 Formosa Avenue

In the early 1920s, this was the Pickford-Fairbanks Studios, where Fairbanks made his classics *Robin Hood* and *The Thief of Bagdad*. Later it became Goldwyn Studios, and since 1980 it has been owned by Warner Bros. and used for the production of both motion pictures and television programs. Quinn Martin's shows, including "Barnaby Jones," "Cannon," and "The Fugitive," were all filmed here, as were "Love Boat," "Dynasty," and the features *Volcano, Basic Instinct, Mars Attacks!, My Fellow*

Americans, Species and *Dangerous Minds*. The studio's Goldwyn Sound Facilities, which provided the postproduction sound for *Star Wars, Raiders of the Lost Ark* and the *Rocky* pictures, is arguably the most prestigious sound department in the business. No tours; visitors are not allowed.

7. FORMOSA CAFE, 7156 Santa Monica Boulevard, (213) 850-9050

This famed Chinese/American restaurant was once frequented by Marilyn Monroe, Humphrey Bogart and Clark Gable.

8. HOME AT 8983 NORMA PLACE

Humorist Dorothy Parker lived in this white stucco bungalow in the early 1960s; and it was here, on June 14, 1963, that she found her husband, Alan Campbell, dead. According to her biographer Leslie Frewin, in *The Late Mrs. Dorothy Parker*, a neighbor asked Parker: "Dottie, tell me, dear. What can I do to help you?" Parker answered: "get me a new husband." When the neighbor said how appalled she was by Parker's remark, Parker reportedly made her famous remark: "Sorry. Then run down to the corner and get me a ham and cheese on rye and tell them to hold the mayo." (Incidentally, Norma Place is named after actress Norma Talmadge, who built a studio on the street. Dolly Parton owns a house on this street.)

9. THE SPORTS CONNECTION, 8612 Santa Monica Boulevard

This is the gymnasium where the John Travolta-Jamie Lee Curtis movie *Perfect* was filmed.

10. MORTON'S, 8800 Melrose Avenue, (310) 276-1253

Studio heads, superagents and their biggest stars often do business over dinner here. Kim Basinger and Alec Baldwin had their first date here.

11. PACIFIC DESIGN CENTER, 8667 Melrose Avenue

Sometimes referred to as "The Blue Whale," the Design Center is the West Coast's largest resource for upscale residential and office furnishings. The building houses more than 200 showrooms to the trade. The building is open to the public; however, purchases must be made through design professionals.

12. CEDARS-SINAI MEDICAL CENTER, 8700 Beverly Boulevard (city of Los Angeles)

Hollywood's Grave Line Tour likes to point out that many celebrities (Danny Kaye, Sammy Davis, Jr., Lucille Ball, Peter Lawford, Jack Warner) died here. Of course, the reason so many stars die here is because it is one of finest hospitals in the country, and dying stars want the best. Michelle Pfeiffer, Mary Hart, Ronald and Nancy Reagan, Michael J. Fox, Michael Jackson, Clint Eastwood, Pierce Brosnan, Jack Nicholson, Warren Beatty and Annette Bening, are among the dozens of other celebrities who have had children delivered here.

13. TAIL O' THE PUP, 329 N. San Vicente Boulevard, (213) 652-4517

In the movie *Ruthless People*, Judge Reinhold made his ransom demands at this fast-food stand, which is shaped like a giant hot dog in a bun. The Pup is considered to be one of Los Angeles' most famous architectural landmarks.

14. BEVERLY CENTER, 8500 Beverly Boulevard at La Cienega Boulevard (city of Los Angeles)

In *Volcano*, the lava flow that was about to engulf this upscale shopping center—and destroy L.A.'s westside—was rerouted when demolition crews blew up a high-rise across the street. (The building was, of course, digitally imposed.)

The Woody Allen-Bette Midler feature *Scenes from a Mall* was supposed to have been set in the Beverly Center (although, with the exception of a few exterior scenes, most of the film was actually filmed at the Stamford Town Center in Stamford, Connecticut.)

On the northwest side of the mall is the famous Hard Rock Cafe, which attracts a young rock crowd.

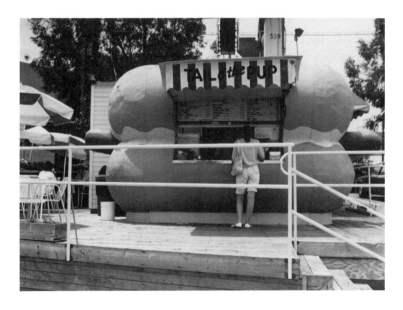

The Tail o' the Pup hot dog stand.

RESTAURANTS IN AND NEAR WEST HOLLY-WOOD WHERE YOU HAVE THE BEST CHANCES OF SEEING SOMEONE FAMOUS:

- DRAI'S, 730 N. La Cienega Boulevard, (310) 358-8585

- THE IVY, 113. N. Robertson Boulevard, (310) 274-8303

- ORSO, 8706 W. Third Street, (310) 274-7144

- LOCANDA VENATA, 8638 W. Third St., (310) 274-1893

- DAN TANA'S, 9071 Santa Monica Boulevard, (310) 275-9444

- THE PALM, 9001 Santa Monica Boulevard, (310) 550-8811

- HUGO'S, 8401 Santa Monica Boulevard, (310) 654-3993

- CICADA, 8478 Melrose Avenue, (213) 655-5559

- ECLIPSE, 8800 Melrose Avenue, (310) 724-5959

- GEORGIA, 7250 Melrose Avenue, (213) 933-8420

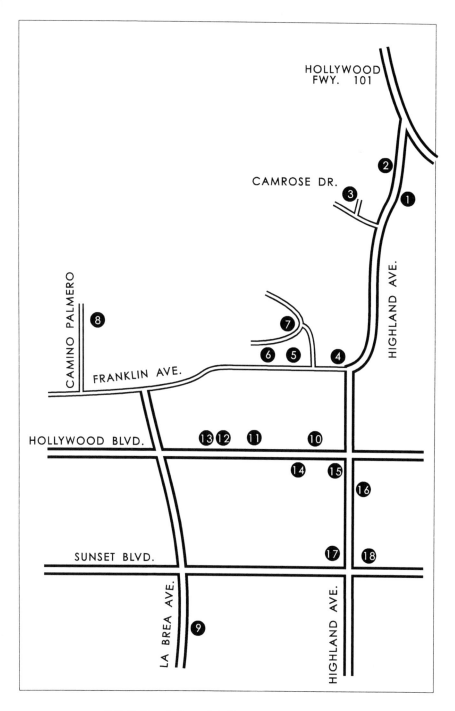

MAP 19 HOLLYWOOD

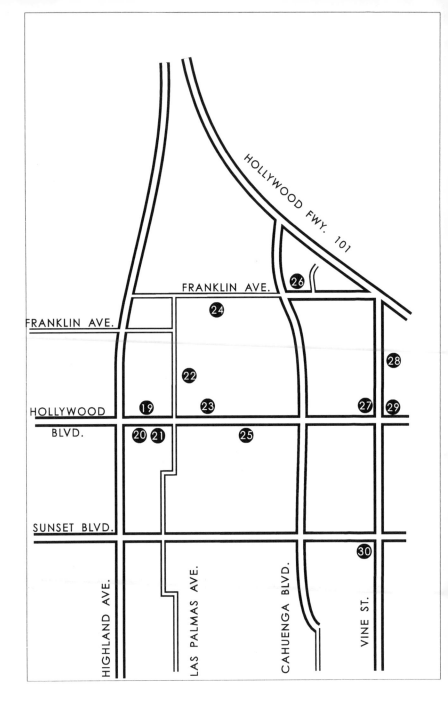

MAP 20 HOLLYWOOD

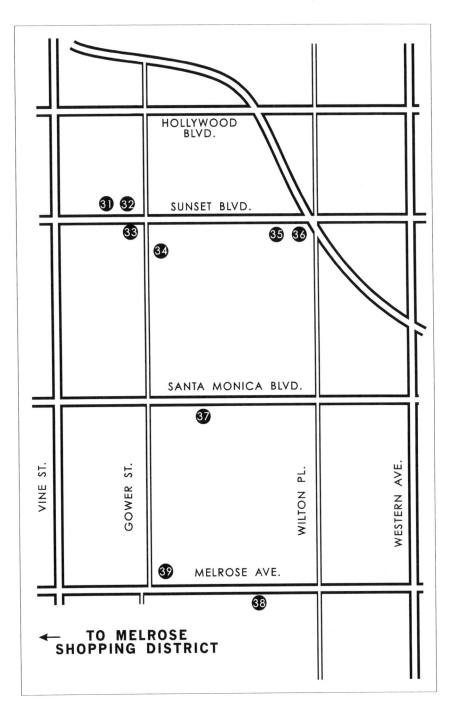

MAP 21 HOLLYWOOD

HOLLYWOOD

1. HOLLYWOOD STUDIO MUSEUM, 2100 N. Highland Avenue

Dedicated to early Hollywood filmmaking, the Hollywood Studio Museum is located in the barn where Cecil B. DeMille directed *The Squaw Man,* the first feature-length film shot entirely in Hollywood. Some books give the erroneous impression that the barn is where the first movie ever filmed was made, but as former museum director Kari Johnson points out, several filmmakers set up shop in Santa Monica and in downtown Los Angeles as early as 1906, eight years before *The Squaw Man's* 1914 release. The movie's "real claim to fame," says Johnson, "is that it was the first nationally successfully feature-length western." Its success also inspired other filmmakers to follow the lead of director DeMille and producer Jesse Lasky and set up shop in Hollywood.

The barn, which was originally located a few miles east of its present site—at the intersection of Selma and Vine Streets—was subsequently moved to Paramount's back lot in 1926, where it was used as the railroad station in "Bonanza." The barn was later donated by Paramount Pictures and the Hollywood Chamber of Commerce to Hollywood Heritage, Inc., which operates the museum. Hours vary during the year; call (213) 874-2276 for information.

2. HOLLYWOOD BOWL, 2301 N. Highland Avenue

Since its opening in 1922, this world-famous outdoor amphitheater has hosted performances by virtually every well-known musician. The Bowl Museum is open daily; call (213) 850-2058 for hours. There is no charge for admission.

3. HIGH TOWER (at the north end of Hightower Drive, west of Camrose Drive)

Fans of the 1991 suspense thriller *Dead Again* will immediately recognize this unusual-looking Italian tower. It was here—and in the studio apartment immediately to the right of it—that the climactic scene played out. The location was deliberately chosen (and even included in the original script) because the producers wanted to show that Emma Thompson, who lived in the apartment adjacent to High Tower, was literally cut off from outside help.

The five-story tower houses an elevator which services the houses and apartments built into the hillside. The elevator is inaccessible to the public, but the area offers some interesting photo possibilities.

Elliott Gould, playing detective Philip Marlowe, lived in the same apartment in the Robert Altman's *The Long Goodbye*.

4. FIRST UNITED METHODIST CHURCH OF HOLLYWOOD, 6817 Franklin Avenue

This is the church where Earthlings sought refuge from invading Martians in the 1952 classic *War of the Worlds*. The "Enchantment Under the Sea" dance in the first two *Back to the Future* movies was filmed here, and *Sister Act* was filmed in several rooms.

5. MAGIC CASTLE, 7001 Franklin Avenue (corner of Orange Drive), (213) 851-3313

This Victorian mansion, completed in 1908, is now an exclusive private club for magicians. You have to be a member or an invited guest to get in.

6. HIGHLAND GARDENS (formerly the Landmark Hotel), 7047 Franklin Avenue (corner of Outpost Drive)

Janis Joplin died of a heroin overdose in room 105 of this Hollywood hotel on October 4, 1970. She was 27.

Hollywood's High Tower, where the climactic scene in *Dead Again* was played out.

7. YAMASHIRO RESTAURANT, 1999 N. Sycamore Avenue, (213) 466-5125

Yamashiro means "mountain palace" and that is what the restaurant is: an exact replica of a Japanese palace located in the Yamashiro mountains near Kyoto, Japan. Standing on a hillside some 250 feet above Hollywood Boulevard, and offering a panoramic view of the city, the restaurant was originally a private estate commissioned by two brothers who sold Oriental antiques. In 1914, hundreds of skilled craftspersons were brought from Japan to duplicate the Yamashiro mansion. The restaurant was later turned into a military school and at one point was converted into apartments where several celebrities, including Richard Pryor and Pernell Roberts, lived. In 1968 Yamashiro was transformed into a restaurant. It served as the officers' club in *Sayonara* starring Marlon Brando, and often doubles as Japan in commercials and television productions. Scenes from the 1992 feature *Man Trouble*, starring Jack Nicholson and Ellen Barkin, were also filmed here.

8. OZZIE AND HARRIET HOUSE, 1822 Camino Palmero

The Nelson family—Ozzie, Harriet, David and Ricky—lived here for over 25 years, and the outside of the house was used in their long-running (1952-66) ABC situation comedy, "The Adventures of Ozzie and Harriet." According to Laurie Jacobson's book *Hollywood Haunted,* subsequent owners claimed the house is haunted by a ghost who would get frisky with the owner's wife. In the early 1930s, movie mogul Sam Goldwyn lived next door at 1800 Camino Palmero, at the corner of Franklin Avenue.

9. A & M RECORDS, 1416 N. La Brea Avenue (just south of Sunset)

A & M are the initials of the last names of the company's founders and former owners, Herb Alpert and Jerry Moss. They bought the studio in 1966, and recorded artists such as Sting, Janet Jackson, Suzanne Vega, Amy Grant, Bryan Adams, and Rita Coolidge. The studio itself was initially built in 1919 by Charlie Chaplin, who made his classics *The Gold Rush, Modern Times, City Lights,* and *The Great Dictator* here. In 1985, 45 top pop stars, including Michael Jackson, Bruce Springsteen, Stevie Wonder, Tina Turner, Cyndi Lauper, Lionel Ritchie, and Diana Ross, recorded "We Are the World" here.

(Note: Rock fans might be interested to know that just off the map—and half a mile west of A & M Records—at 7439 Sunset Boulevard—is the Sunset Grill, the eatery immortalized in Don Henley's song.)

10. MANN'S CHINESE THEATER, 6925 Hollywood Boulevard, (213) 464-8111

The Chinese Theater, which is undoubtedly the most famous theater in the world, opened in 1927 with the premiere of Cecil B. DeMille's *King of Kings.* Its forecourt includes the hand and footprints of almost 200 Hollywood legends—although some have left other trademarks, including Jimmy Durante's nose, Harpo Marx's harp, Sonja Henje's ice skates, Betty Grable's legs, Al Jolson's knee, and Donald Duck's webbed feet. The Mann Theater chain, which bought the theater from showman Sid Grauman, still holds inscription ceremonies. Recent honorees include Jim Carrey, Jackie Chan, Harrison Ford, Mel Gibson, Whoopi Goldberg, Michael Keaton,   Steven   Seagal,   Meryl   Streep,   Arnold Schwarzenegger, Bruce Willis, and all seven members of the original *Star Trek* cast. The 1,492-seat theater also hosted the Academy Awards in 1949.

11. HOLLYWOOD ENTERTAINMENT MUSEUM, 7021 Hollywood Boulevard (at Sycamore)

Hollywood's newest museum has something special for "Star Trek" fans: the bridge of the U.S.S. Enterprise used for the filming of "Star Trek: The Next Generation." Paramount Studios, which donated the set, also donated the set from the long-running NBC sitcom "Cheers," complete with the signatures of the cast members which were carved on the bar after the show's final episode aired in 1993.

The museum, which was created to preserve and celebrate the entertainment industry, also includes a remarkably detailed miniature replica of Hollywood during its golden era; a Max Factor fashion and make-up exhibit where tourists can be made over like the stars; a collection of historical camera equipment; various interactive exhibits; a backlot, which includes studio costumes and props; a foley room, where visitors are taught to create their own sound effects; and an electronic library which features access to Internet entertainment sites and job opportunities in the industry.

The museum is open Tuesdays through Sundays from 10:00 A.M. to 6:00 P.M., with special educational events, including screenings and lectures, held during evening hours. For prices call (213) 465-7900.

12. THE HOLLYWOOD WALK OF FAME

Conceived by the Hollywood Chamber of Commerce in the late 1950s as a tribute to artists who have made significant contributions to the film, radio, television and recording industries, the Walk of Fame is also a

147

promotional tool used by celebrities to plug their new movies, albums and concert tours. The "honor" costs $7,500 and is not always paid for by the stars. For example, Liza Minelli's fan club held bake sales to pay for her star. The selection process has generated some controversy. Blake Edwards, Valerie Harper, Dr. Joyce Brothers and Suzanne Somers have all had requests for stars turned down. Some major stars—Dustin Hoffman, Clint Eastwood, Meryl Streep, George C. Scott, Jane Fonda, Sidney Poitier, Warren Beatty and Peter O'Toole,

A premiere at the world-famous Mann's Chinese Theater, circa 1964.

among others—have never bothered vying for the honor. The Walk, which now includes some 2,100 stars, and which extends from Hollywood Boulevard between LaBrea and Gower Street, and Vine Street between Sunset Boulevard and Yucca Street, is a popular tourist site. If you are in town, call the Hollywood Chamber of Commerce at (213) 469-8311 for a schedule of their forthcoming induction ceremonies.

Tom Selleck's star on the Walk of Fame.

13. FILM PERMIT OFFICE (ENTERTAINMENT INDUSTRY DEVELOPMENT CORPORATION), 7083 Hollywood Boulevard, Fifth Floor

A location scout once remarked to me: "It's funny how tourists, hoping to see how movies are made, always go to Universal Studios. If they really want to see how movies are made, they should go to the permit office [two blocks from Mann's Chinese Theater] and pick up the shoot sheets. Then they can see for themselves how boring moviemaking is!"

Tourists who have never seen a movie being filmed may not find moviemaking as boring as jaded Angelinos do, and if they want to know what is filming around town, the film permit office has the answers. The office makes available to the general public a list—or shoot sheet—of all the motion pictures, television programs, commercials and videos being filmed that day outside the studios and within the city limits of Los Angeles. The shoot sheets, which are free, provide the name of the production, the address where filming is taking place, and the time of day for which the permits are issued. Unfortunately, the shoot sheets do not tell whether the crews are filming indoors or outdoors (if crews are filming inside a house or building, chances are you will not see anything). To take full advantage of the shoot sheet one also has to be knowledgeable about the different projects being filmed. The two Hollywood trade papers, *Daily Variety* and *The Hollywood Reporter,* print production charts which tell you who the director and cast members of movies are; so if you buy the trades on the right days and cross-reference the production charts with the information on the shoot sheets you can increase your chances of going to a site where a major movie is being filmed. Many tourists, of course, do not have the time to do all this; so if you want to take full advantage of the shoot sheets, find a film buff or an independent tour guide who knows his or her way around the city.

14. HOLLYWOOD ROOSEVELT HOTEL, 7000 Hollywood Boulevard, (213) 466-7000.

The hotel's Blossom Room was the site of the first Academy Awards ceremony in 1929. That year the awards were called the Merit Awards and Janet Gaynor and Emil Jennings were honored as best actor and actress, while *Wings* took honors as best feature.

The hotel's nightclub, the Cinegrill, offers performances from well-known singers, and, along with Blossom Room and the hotel lobby, has been a site for location filming. The strip tease show in *Beverly Hills Cop II* as well as a few of Michelle Pfeiffer's nightclub scenes in *The Fabulous Baker Boys* were filmed in the Cinegrill. *Boiling Point,* which starred Wesley Snipes and Dennis Hopper, filmed extensively throughout the hotel. The Roosevelt's mezzanine includes a photographic exhibit tracing the history of Hollywood.

15. EL CAPITAN THEATER, 6838 Hollywood Boulevard (corner Orchid), (213) 467-7674

This Art Deco movie palace, which was restored in 1991, is one of Hollywood's architectural jewels. It is also the venue for Disney world premieres and the highest grossing single screen theater in the country.

16. FUTURE SITE OF THE HOLLYWOOD HISTORY MUSEUM, 1666 N. Highland Avenue

The museum is expected to open in 1999, with details to be announced. The Art Deco building, which once housed the Max Factor Museum, was dressed up for

Beverly Hills Cop II and used as the exterior of the jewelry store, Adriano's, robbed by Brigitte Nielsen.

17. HOLLYWOOD HIGH SCHOOL, 1521 N. Highland Avenue

Until Hollywood declined in the mid-1960s, Hollywood High—and its drama department—served as sort of an unofficial actor's training ground for the studios. The school's alumni include Jason Robards, James Garner, Carol Burnett, Sally Kellerman, Stephanie Powers, Linda Evans, John Ritter, Jean Peters, Rick and David Nelson, Fay Wray, Mickey Rooney, Judy Garland, Nanette Fabray, Alan Hale, Yvette Mimieux, Tuesday Weld, Swoozie Kurtz, Meredith Baxter Birney, Barbara Hershey, Ruta Lee, Swoosie Kurtz, Mike Farrell, Charlene Tilton, Denise Crosby, Scott Baio, Tim Burton, Rita Wilson, Ione Skye, Donovan Leitch and Brandy.

In *Hollywood High: The History of America's Most Famous Public (High) School*, John Blumenthal writes that Hollywood High started going downhill in 1968 when the Los Angeles school board drastically shrank the Hollywood district boundaries: "As a result, upper-middle-class areas like Toluca Lake and Studio City, which had once sent their children to Hollywood High, were suddenly located in another district. 'That was the turning point,' observed Hollywood High English teacher Harry Major in the pages of *The News*. 'In one blow, we lost the cream of our students.'" By the mid-1970s, Blumenthal writes: "most recent alumni were clerk-typists, salespeople, factory workers, or stenographers."

18. FORMER SITE OF THE TOP HAT CAFE, 1500 N. Highland Avenue (northeast corner of Highland and Sunset)

It was at a malt shop once located at this site, not at Schwab's Pharmacy, that Lana Turner, then a student at Hollywood High, was "discovered" and turned into star. Turner told *Los Angeles Times* columnist Jack Smith that she cut a typing class and was in the shop when she was approached by nightclub owner and *Hollywood Reporter* publisher Billy Wilkerson, who asked her: "How would you like to be in the movies?" Turner said her response was: "I don't know—I'll have to ask my mother."

19. HOLLYWOOD WAX MUSEUM, 6767 Hollywood Boulevard, (213) 462-8860

20. GUINNESS WORLD RECORDS MUSEUM, 6764 Hollywood Boulevard, (213) 463-6433

21. EGYPTIAN THEATER, 6712 Hollywood Boulevard (at Las Palmas Avenue), (213) 467-6167

Built by Sid Grauman in 1922, five years before the opening of the Chinese Theater, this was Hollywood's first movie palace. One of the more architecturally unusual buildings in Hollywood, the Egyptian was originally planned with a Spanish motif, but was redesigned with an Egyptian theme after King Tut's tomb was discovered. It is now the headquarters of American Cinematheque, a nonprofit cultural group dedicated to filmmaking heritage.

22. "*PRETTY WOMAN*" HOTEL, 1738 N. Las Palmas Avenue (at Yucca Street)

In *Pretty Woman*, Julia Roberts lived—and was eventually rescued by Richard Gere—at the Las Palmas Hotel. (Note: Walking around this neighborhood at night or alone is not recommended.)

23. MUSSO AND FRANK GRILL, 6667 Hollywood Boulevard, (213) 467-7788 or (213) 467-5123

While Musso and Frank pride themselves for being the oldest extant restaurant in Hollywood, it is, more importantly, the only one on Hollywood Boulevard still frequented by entertainment industry types. The restaurant was seen in the opening credits of the short-lived television show about a young Hollywood agent, "The Fabulous Teddy Z," and in the movie *Ed Wood*. Director Tim Burton filmed a scene in which Wood, who is regarded by many as the most inept director in movie history, met one of the most famous, Orson Welles.

24. MONTECITO APARTMENTS, 6650 Franklin Avenue (at Cherokee Avenue)

Ronald Reagan rented an apartment at the Montecito when he first moved to Hollywood. He lived here between 1937 and 1939, while working as a contract player for Warner Bros. Mickey Rooney, George C. Scott, Julie Harris, and Gene Hackman also lived in this former resident hotel, which is now an apartment building for senior citizens and handicapped people.

25. FREDERICK'S OF HOLLYWOOD LINGERIE MUSEUM, 6608 Hollywood Boulevard, (213) 466-8506

This Art Deco building is the flagship store of Frederick's and features a Celebrity Lingerie Hall of Fame which salutes stars of stage, screen and television who "glamorized" lingerie. The museum exhibits a Madonna bustier, a Judy Garland nightie, a Phyllis Diller training bra, and the first dress Milton Berle wore on television.

26. ALTO-NIDO APARTMENTS, 1851 N. Ivar Avenue (two blocks north of Hollywood Boulevard at Franklin)

In the classic feature film *Sunset Boulevard*, William Holden, playing unemployed screenwriter Joe Gillis, lived at the Alto-Nido Apartments.

27. CORNER OF HOLLYWOOD AND VINE

Although the legend of Hollywood and Vine lives on, the only things there today of even remotely passing interest are the Walk of Fame stars saluting Apollo XI astronauts Neil Armstrong, Edward Aldrin, Jr., and Michael Collins. The astronauts were honored not for being the first men to journey to the moon, but because they appeared in an "outstanding television production"!

Beyond that, all the intersection has to offer are office buildings, a fast-food pizzeria, and a combination souvenir/convenience store. *Los Angeles Times* columnist Jack Smith opined that the corner "must be a letdown to [the millions of movie worshipers] who make the pilgrimage. It is the main corner of Anyplace, U.S.A."

Why then does Hollywood and Vine live on in the imaginations of movie fans? Well, back in the 1920s and 1930s, broadcasters used to announce that their programs originated from "Hollywood and Vine." At the time, most of the major studios—Paramount, Fox, Columbia, and Warner Bros., as well as NBC and other radio stations, many theaters and restaurants—were all located within a few blocks of the intersection.

"That's why Hollywood and Vine became famous," says Hollywood Studio Museum executive director Richard Adkins. "So many stars were working and spending their free time there."

28. CAPITOL RECORDS, 1750 N. Vine Street

The Capitol Tower, which was designed in 1954, is one of Hollywood's most identifiable landmarks. It is a circular office building resembling a stack of records with a needle on top (although the architect, Welton Becket, denies that he created the look intentionally). Capitol's artists over the years have included Frank Sinatra, Nat "King" Cole, the Beatles, the Beach Boys, Tina Turner, Donnie Osmond, the Doobie Brothers, Heart, Hammer, and the Steve Miller Band. The company's Gold Awards are on display in the lobby, but the company does not offer tours for the public.

29. PANTAGES THEATER, 6233 Hollywood Boulevard (just east of Vine), (213) 480-3232

Another extraordinary example of Art Deco architecture, the Pantages was the site of the Academy Awards in the 1950s.

30. CINERAMA DOME, 6360 Sunset Boulevard (corner of Ivar Avenue, one block west of Vine Street), (213) 466-3401

The Cinerama movie craze—in which movies were presented on three screens to give the moviegoer the illusion of being engaged in the action—died in the 1960s, but this geodesic-domed theater, built exclusively for those films, lives on as a conventional movie theater.

The Capitol Records Tower, one of Hollywood's most famous
landmarks.

31. HOLLYWOOD PALLADIUM, 6215 Sunset Boulevard, (213) 466-4311

Once the world's largest dance club, the Palladium has hosted Emmy, Grammy and Golden Globe Awards. "The Lawrence Welk Show" was also broadcast from here for years.

32. CHANNEL 2 KCBS, 6121 Sunset Boulevard (between El Centro Avenue and Gower Street)

The first motion picture studio in Hollywood—the Nestor Film Company—was originally located on this site. Nestor later merged with Universal Studios. In 1938 CBS built Columbia Square Complex, which houses Los Angeles' channel 2 and the CBS-owned radio station KNX.

33. GOWER GULCH, 6098 Sunset Boulevard (at Gower Street)

During the late teens and early 1920s, a number of independent studios—many of them fly-by-nights—operated in this stretch of Sunset Boulevard, and extras looking for work used to hang out in this area. Many came dressed in costume as cowboys and Indians, and someone named the area "Gower Gulch." To pay homage to that era the developers of the shopping center designed it to resemble a Western street.

34. SUNSET-GOWER STUDIOS, 1438 N. Gower Street

Once the home of Columbia Studios (now located in Culver City), Sunset-Gower is now a privately owned rental studio used mostly for television filming. When you drive by, you will see billboards with the names of the shows currently taping on the lot.

(Note: The next two entries are both four blocks east on Sunset. To reach Hollywood Memorial Cemetery, go south on Gower Street and west on Santa Monica Boulevard.)

35. KTLA, 5858 Sunset Boulevard (between Bronson and Van Ness)

This neo-colonial mansion was the original home of Warner Bros. and the site of the 1927 filming of *The Jazz Singer*, the first feature film which featured synchronized dialogue. When Warner moved its main headquarters to Burbank in 1929, this facility was used to produce "Bugs Bunny," "Porky Pig," and other Warner animated cartoons. Today the building houses the independent television station KTLA (Los Angeles' channel 5) and radio station KTZN. KTLA does not offer a tour.

36. FOX TELEVISION CENTER, 5746 Sunset Boulevard

This is the home of KTTV (channel 11 in Los Angeles). Some of the offices of Fox Broadcasting Company—which are also located on the 20th Century Fox lot—are located here.

37. HOLLYWOOD MEMORIAL PARK CEMETERY, 6000 Santa Monica Boulevard (between Bronson and Van Ness Avenues)

Many of Hollywood's early greats (Rudolph Valentino, Charlie Chaplin, Mary Pickford, Cecil B. DeMille, Tyrone Power, and Douglas Fairbanks, Sr.) are buried here. So are Peter Finch, Peter Lorre, Carl "Alfalfa" Switzer, director John Huston, and Harry Cohn, the much-despised former president of Columbia Pictures. Legend has it that the reason Cohn's funeral was so well-attended was that many of those present wanted to make sure that he was dead.

For years a mysterious veiled "Lady in Black" brought flowers to Rudolph Valentino's tomb on the anniversary of Valentino's death. The Jewish section of the cemetery features the graves of mobster Bugsy Siegel as well as Mel Blanc, the voice of Bugs Bunny and Porky Pig, whose epitaph reads: "That's all, folks."

Visiting hours are 8:00 A.M. to 5:00 P.M. throughout the grounds. Maps of the stars' graves are available at the main entrance for those wishing to tour the site.

38. RALEIGH STUDIOS, 650 N. Bronson Avenue (on both the southeast and southwest corners of Melrose)

Raleigh may or may not be the oldest continually operating studio in Hollywood (KCET makes the same claim, and the dispute is probably over the word "continually"). In any event, it is a rental studio used primarily for commercials, although some television shows, feature films, and music videos have also filmed here. When the studio was called the Producers' Studio in the 1960s, Ronald Reagan hosted "Death Valley Days" here. Episodes from "The Life of Riley," "Gunsmoke," "The Adventures of Superman," "Perry Mason," and "Have Gun, Will Travel" were also filmed on the lot. Not open to the public.

39. PARAMOUNT STUDIOS, 5555 Melrose Avenue

Paramount is the only major studio that has not fled Hollywood for the suburbs. One of its main attractions is its famous wrought-iron side gate, at the corner of Bronson

Mel Blanc's grave at Hollywood Memorial Cemetery.

The Paramount Studios gate.

Avenue and Marathon Street—which is not to be confused with the main gate on Melrose. The side gate was immortalized in *Sunset Boulevard* and has appeared in countless other movies.

Although the studio does not extensively promote their tour ("we do not want it to get too large or too disruptive; we do it more as a public service," says a studio spokesman), the studio does offer a two-hour walking tour of its lot. The tour, which starts at the side entrance of the studio at 860 N. Gower Street, is conducted three times daily, Monday through Friday, at 9:00 A.M., 11:00 A.M. and 2:00 P.M., and costs a reasonable $15. Visitors are walked through the back lot, shown how various studio departments operate, and sometimes given the opportunity to watch rehearsals of television shows. The rehearsal-watching is not guaranteed. The chances of seeing a show being rehearsed are much greater in the late spring or summer, when shows are in production, and not possible at all when the shows are on hiatus, usually during the Christmas holiday. It is also possible to get tickets to see shows produced by Paramount. For tickets and additional tour information, call Paramount Guest Relations at (213) 956-5575.

(Note: After driving past Paramount you have a number of options for additional touring. You can make a left turn onto Rossmore Avenue and do the Hancock Park/Wilshire District tour—or you can continue west on Melrose for about a mile and a half until you reach La Brea. Between La Brea and Fairfax is the world-famous Melrose Avenue shopping district, which is the only place in the world where you will find stores with names like Wacko, Condomania, Street Legal, and Retail Slut.

Melrose is a popular hangout among yuppies and punk rockers.

The television show "Melrose Place" sometimes films on Melrose Avenue; but do not go looking for the apartment building there. For exterior shots, the producers used an apartment building in Los Feliz (see page 195). The interior courtyard, including the pool area, and the interiors of the apartments, exist only on a studio backlot in the city of Santa Clarita, some thirty miles north of Los Angeles.

Also not on the map—and a few blocks out of the way—is another rental studio, Hollywood Center Studios, 1040 N. Las Palmas Avenue, located two blocks east of Highland and north of Melrose—before the Melrose shopping district. There is not much to see from the outside, but just about everything has filmed on the lot: features [*Con Air, Misery,* and *When Harry Met Sally*], games shows ["Jeopardy"], weekly television series ["I Love Lucy," "The Adventures of Ozzie and Harriet," "Get Smart," "Mr. Ed," and "The Beverly Hillbillies"], commercials, and music videos, including some by Michael Jackson. The studio does not offer a tour of its facilities.)

Perched atop a small hill which overlooks the Hollywood Freeway, Castle Ivar (2061 Ivar Avenue) seems ready to withstand an army of armor clad invaders.

CELEBRITIES WHO OWN HOMES IN HOLLY-WOOD: No celebrities live in the Hollywood "flats," but a number live in the fashionable hills north of Hollywood Boulevard. Bob Barker, Alyce Beasley, Ken Berry, Ruth Buzzi, Beverly D'Angelo, Rebecca DeMornay, Melissa Etheridge, Brian Austin Greene, Howard Hesseman, Ken Kerchival, Penny Marshall, Lou Diamond Phillips, Andrew Shue, and Gore Vidal own homes in the prestigious Outpost Estates, by Outpost Drive.

Kathleen Beller, Thomas Dolby, and Michelle Green live in Whitley Heights, a community north of Highland and east of Franklin Avenue (behind the Hollywood Studio Museum) where many of the stars of the silent era once lived.

Ned Beatty, Peter Bonerz, Sandra Bullock, Terence Knox, Gates McFadden, Paul Reubens (formerly known as Pee-Wee Herman), Marina Sirtis, Ione Skye, Jodi Watley, Paul Winfield, and Neil Young have homes in "Hollywoodland"—the Hollywood Hills east of Highland Avenue.

Johnny Cochran, Lorenzo Lamas, Madonna, Dermot Mulroney, Brad Pitt, Annie Potts, Alexander Siddig, Lily Tomlin, Nana Visitor, and Stevie Wonder live in Los Feliz, an exclusive neighborhood of grand older houses south of Griffith Park.

165

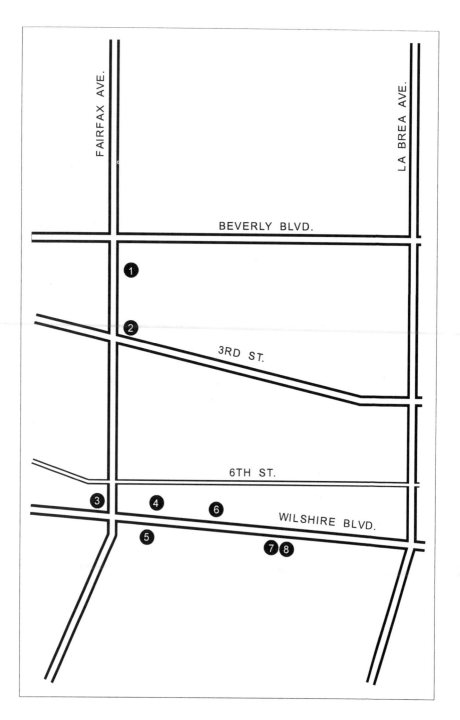

MAP 22 FAIRFAX AND THE MIRACLE MILE

FAIRFAX AND
THE MIRACLE MILE

1. CBS TELEVISION CITY, 7800 Beverly Boulevard (at Fairfax Avenue)

CBS does not offer a tour of its facility, but tickets for "Family Feud," "Wheel of Fortune," "The Price is Right," and other programs airing on the network are available by calling (213) 852-2458. CBS also has a walk-up ticket booth open 9:00 A.M. to 5:00 P.M., where you can pick up tickets for shows filming that evening.

2. FARMER'S MARKET, 3rd Street and Fairfax Avenue, (213) 933-9211

The *Los Angeles Times* placed Farmer's Market at the top of its list of the ten best places to spot celebrities in L.A. The *Times* reported that: "A wide spectrum of celebs is known to meander through the stalls, from John Malkovich and Michelle Pfeiffer to Mickey Rooney and Doris Day. The young crowd eats at Kokomos, the older ones are there to shop. The soap opera stars from CBS are there to grab lunch."

3. JOHNIE'S RESTAURANT, 6101 Wilshire Boulevard (at Fairfax Avenue), (213) 938-3521

The 1989 thriller *Miracle Mile* told the story of a musician and his girlfriend who learned of an impending nuclear strike and tried to escape Hollywood before the missiles hit. The musician in the movie, Anthony

Edwards, learned of the attack at a phone booth outside this restaurant.

Johnie's was destroyed in *Volcano*, along with most of the Wilshire corridor. The restaurant was also featured in *Reservoir Dogs* and was where Lily Tomlin waitressed in *Short Cuts*.

4. LOS ANGELES COUNTY MUSEUM OF ART, 5905 Wilshire Boulevard, (213) 857-6000

The museum has appeared in several movies, including *L.A. Story*, in which Steve Martin, a real-life avid art collector, was the only one in a foursome to see a naked woman in a work of abstract art. In *The Player*, Cher and dozens of other celebrities, playing themselves, attended a gala studio event. Featuring some of the country's best art, the museum is worth a visit. The museum is closed on Mondays but is open Tuesdays through Thursdays from 10:00 A.M. to 5:00, Fridays from 10:00 A.M. to 9:00 P.M., and Saturdays and Sundays from 11:00 to 6:00 P.M.

5. MUTUAL BENEFIT LIFE BUILDING, 5900 Wilshire Boulevard

This 31-story-tall building is the site from which Anthony Edwards desperately tried to arrange a helicopter get-away in *Miracle Mile*. The helicopter landed on the roof of the building, and Edwards and Mare Winningham got as far as the La Brea Tar Pits across the street.

6. LA BREA TAR PITS AND THE GEORGE C. PAGE MUSEUM OF LA BREA DISCOVERIES, 5801 Wilshire Boulevard, (213) 857-6301

The Pits are pools of asphaltum and crude oil that have trapped more than 200 varieties of birds, mammals, plants, reptiles and insects, some dating back to prehistoric times. While the Pits were ground zero for the eruption in *Volcano*, scientists assure us that the only real-life dangers lurking beneath the Pits are L.A.'s crazy quilt of earthquake faults.

7. WILSHIRE COURTYARD, 5750 and 5750 Wilshire Boulevard

Twin office buildings which house (in addition to banks and attorneys' offices) *TV Guide, Daily Variety, Us* magazine, and several production companies, including Aaron Spelling's. Spelling, the producer of "Melrose Place," used the courtyard for the exterior shots of D & D Advertising.

8. HEADQUARTERS OF E! ENTERTAINMENT TELEVISION, 5670 Wilshire Boulevard

This is the corporate headquarters and production studios of the cable network, which presents news and features about the entertainment world and its major celebrities. The channel is available in 20 million American homes.

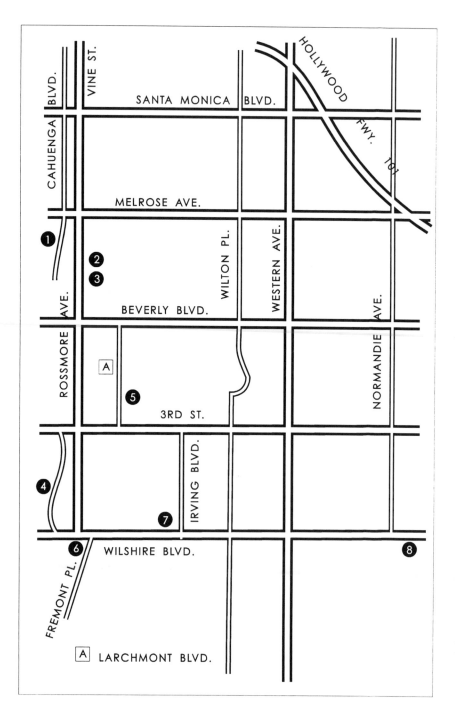

MAP 23 HANCOCK PARK & WILSHIRE DISTRICT

HANCOCK PARK AND THE WILSHIRE DISTRICT

1. **"HAPPY DAYS" HOME,** 565 N. Cahuenga Avenue (south of Melrose Avenue)

   Served as the Cunningham home in the long-running (1974-84) ABC sitcom "Happy Days."

2. **FORMER HOME OF MAE WEST,** 570 N. Rossmore Avenue

   For 48 years (from 1932 until her death in 1980), Mae West lived in the penthouse of the Ravenswood Apartments.

3. **EL ROYALE APARTMENTS,** 450 N. Rossmore Avenue (at Rosewood Avenue)

   For years a story circulated that John F. Kennedy stayed here during the 1960 Democratic National Convention in Los Angeles, even though his official campaign headquarters was at the Biltmore Hotel downtown. Sandra Griffin, the El Royale's property manager, checked into the stories, and reported that JFK did not stay at the El Royale, but stayed in room 301 at an apartment building (formerly a hotel, the Rossmore House) two doors down the street—at 522 N. Rossmore Avenue. The book *Johnny, We Hardly Knew Ye* by former JFK aides Kenneth P. O'Donnell and David F. Powers with Joe McCarthy, confirms this, saying that Powers found the hideaway apartment so JFK could "sleep and eat a quiet breakfast, away from the turmoil at the Biltmore."

Tour buses which drive past the El Royale can continue to note it as a point of interest, though. Several celebrities have lived there at one time or another, including Harry Cohn, the former president of Columbia Pictures; William Frawley, who played Fred on "I Love Lucy;" George Raft; Loretta Young; Nicolas Cage; and Clark Gable, who lived here with his second wife, Ria, in 1933.

The lobby of the building was seen in *Switch* starring Ellen Barkin and in *Other People's Money*, where it served as Penelope Anne Miller's apartment.

4. FORMER NAT KING COLE HOME, 401 Muirfield Road

Cole bought this English Tudor mansion in 1948 as a wedding present for his bride, Maria, shocking and angering his WASPy neighbors, who were not used to having blacks around. According to *Lamparski's Hidden Hollywood*, by Richard Lamparski: "Larchmont residents called a property owners' meeting shortly after the Coles moved in. An attorney for the group summed up its feelings when he said that many of those present were born and raised in Larchmont: 'We are greatly disturbed at the prospect of having undesirables living here.' Cole responded: 'I'm relieved to hear how concerned you all are about your neighborhood. I feel exactly the same way. I'd like you all to know that if my wife or I see anyone undesirable in Larchmont we'll be the first to object. Thank you.'"

(Other notables who lived on Muirfield include Howard Hughes, whose first Los Angeles home was at 211; Buster Keaton, who owned a home at 543; and Dan Blocker who lived at 555 Muirfield Road.)

5. MRX PHARMACY, 150 N. Larchmont Boulevard

During the first two seasons of "MacGyver"—when the show was filmed in Los Angeles in 1985 and 1986—Richard Dean Anderson (MacGyver) lived in the loft above the pharmacy. Many of the chase scenes from the Keystone Cop comedies were also filmed on Larchmont.

6. 119 FREMONT PLACE, between 4400 and 4500 Wilshire Boulevard

This was Michael Douglas and Kathleen Turner's home in *War of the Roses.* The house is in a gated community and is not visible from the street.

(Fremont Place has always attracted celebrities. Muhammed Ali lived for years at 55 Fremont Place; Mary Pickford and her mother lived across the street at 56; and Cliff Robertson lived at 97 Fremont Place when the David Begelman scandal broke. Mick Jagger also lived on Fremont Place in the mid-1980s. Sylvester Stallone's house in *Rocky,* according to location manager Mike Alvarado, was also on this street.)

7. SITE OF THE "SUNSET BOULEVARD" MANSION (northwest corner of Wilshire and Irving Boulevards)

An office building with the address 4155 Wilshire Boulevard is now at this site, but in 1950 the mansion in which Gloria Swanson lived in the classic *Sunset Boulevard,* stood here. The mansion once belonged to billionaire J. Paul Getty and was also featured in *Rebel Without a Cause.*

8. AMBASSADOR HOTEL, 3400 Wilshire Boulevard

The Ambassador was once a Hollywood hot spot and is perhaps best known as the site where Robert F. Kennedy was assassinated while running for the presidency in 1968. The hotel closed in 1990 and is today used exclusively for location filming. In addition to playing itself in Tom Hanks' directorial debut, *That Thing You Do!*, the Ambassador was the nightclub in *The Mask*, the Nashville bar where Robin Wright stripped in *Forrest Gump*, the site of *Romy and Michele's High School Reunion*, Gary Sinise and Kevin Bacon's apartments in *Apollo 13*, L'Idiot Restaurant in *L.A. Story*, the Brown Derby restaurant in *Ed Wood*, the hotel Meryl Streep stayed at in *Defending Your Life*, and both a Catskill resort and a glitzy Las Vegas showroom in Billy Crystal's *Mr. Saturday Night*.

The Academy Awards were presented in the hotel's famous Cocoanut Grove six times between 1930 and 1943. In 1947 Marilyn Monroe started as a model at the Emmaline Snively's Blue Book Modeling Agency, located at the hotel.

The property is closed to the public.

JUST OFF THE MAP are a few sites which certainly are not must-sees for tourists who are in Los Angeles for just a short time, but which are worth pointing out if you happen to be driving east on Wilshire Boulevard on your way toward downtown. The first, at 757 New Hampshire Avenue, just south of Wilshire, is the apartment building depicted as Jerry Seinfeld's apartment in the hit sitcom "Seinfeld." That building is only a few blocks from the Bryson Apartment Hotel, located at 2701 Wilshire Boulevard, at the corner of Lafayette Park Place. The Bryson was featured in Raymond Chandler's novel

The Lady of the Lake and was where John Cusack lived in *The Grifters*.

Just east of that is MacArthur Park, which borders 6th and 7th Streets on the north, and Park View on the east and Alvarado Street on the west. Richard Harris immortalized the park in his hit song "MacArthur Park." The area is not one a tourist would go to; it is one of the more dangerous areas in town.

Overlooking MacArthur Park, at 607 S. Park View Street (at the corner of Sixth Street), is the Park Plaza Hotel, which is frequently used as a film location. Ricardo Montalban's office in *The Naked Gun*, the party scene in *Less Than Zero,* the site of the Richard Nixon-Mao Tse Tung meeting in *Nixon*, and Whitney Houston's arrival at the Academy Award ceremonies in *The Bodyguard* were all filmed in or outside the hotel. The hotel has also appeared in *Romy and Michele's High School Reunion, Buffy the Vampire Slayer,* and *Bugsy*.

CELEBRITIES WHO LIVE IN HANCOCK PARK OR NEARBY: Brooke Adams, Jason Alexander, Angela Bassett, Mr. Blackwell, Dixie Carter and Hal Holbrook, James Ingram, John Malkovich, Richard Mulligan, Elizabeth Perkins, Lou Rawls, Julia Sweeney, George Takei, and Julie Warner.

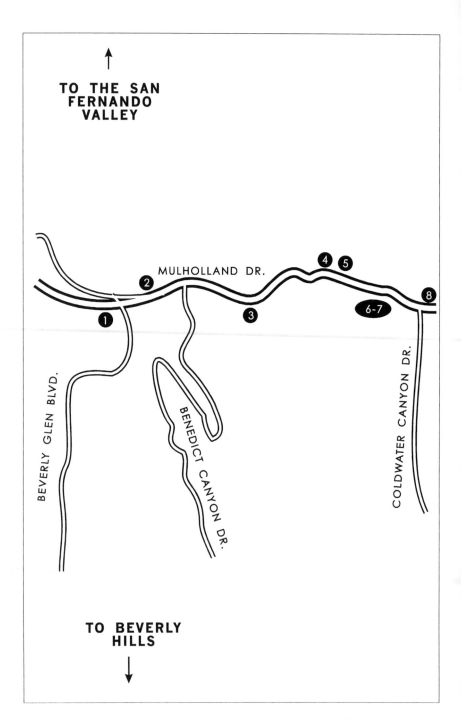

MAP 24 HOLLYWOOD HILLS

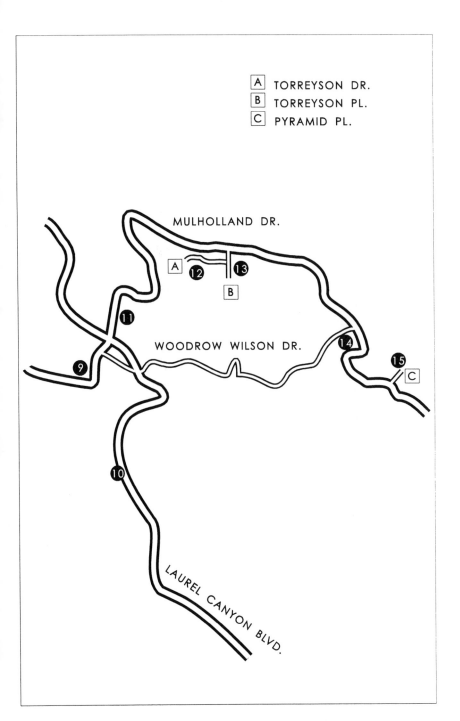

A TORREYSON DR.
B TORREYSON PL.
C PYRAMID PL.

MULHOLLAND DR.

A ❶❷ B ❶❸

❶❶

WOODROW WILSON DR.

❶❹

❶❺
C

❾

❿

LAUREL CANYON BLVD.

MAP 25 HOLLYWOOD HILLS

MULHOLLAND DRIVE AND THE HOLLYWOOD HILLS

A visit to Los Angeles would not be complete without a drive on Mulholland Drive—a windy mountain road which offers breathtaking views of the city and the San Fernando Valley, particularly at night.

Because it is so curvy, Mulholland demands your constant attention. If you make one little mistake, you can drive your car off a cliff—just like they do in the movies (although most of the cliff crash scenes are actually done in the Angeles National Forest north of Los Angeles. Mulholland is more famous for its scenes of lovemaking at the turn-off points which offer the best vantage points of the Valley.)

Since Mulholland does demand your attention, sightseeing by car is not recommended—if you are alone. Of course, if someone else is driving, keep your eyes posted for the following landmarks.

This tour starts by Beverly Glen Boulevard (north of Beverly Hills and Bel-Air) and continues eastward until Mulholland ends by Cahuenga Boulevard—which is north of Hollywood and just west of the Hollywood Freeway.

1. **SANTO PIETRO'S PIZZA**, 2954 Beverly Glen Centre, (213) 474-4349 (off Beverly Glen Boulevard, one-half block south of Mulholland)

Vanna White's husband, George Santo Pietro, owns this restaurant, which is often frequented by many of

178

the celebrities who live on Mulholland. Warren Beatty met Annette Bening here.

2. MULHOLLAND ESTATES, 14111 Mulholland Drive (north side of street, between Beverly Glen Boulevard and Benedict Canyon Drive)

Exclusive gated community where Loni Anderson, Fred Dryer, Paula Abdul, Vanna White and John Fogerty own homes. (Eagles star Don Henley lived in a house across the street. His home is not, however, visible from the street.)

3. BEVERLY PARK (north entrance by 13100 Mulholland Drive)

The most exclusive of the private communities in Los Angeles; it is where Magic Johnson, Denzel Washington, Sasha Stallone, Pia Zadora, Rod Stewart, Richard and Lili Zanuck, Alan Thicke, drummer Alex Van Halen, and Jon Peters have (or are building) homes.

4. HOME OF WARREN BEATTY, 13671 Mulholland Drive

This is not visible from the street.

5. FORMER HOME OF BRUCE WILLIS AND DEMI MOORE, 13511 Mulholland Drive

This is also not visible from the street. Bruce and Demi now divide their time between homes in Malibu, Manhattan, and Idaho.

6. JACK NICHOLSON'S HOME, 12850 Mulholland Drive

This is where, in Nicholson's absence, director Roman Polanski seduced a 13-year-old model, leading to a

Jack Nicholson's home on Mulholland Drive.

1977 charge of unlawful sexual intercourse to which Polanski pleaded guilty. Polanski spent 42 days undergoing psychiatric observation at Chino State Prison; and then, to avoid further jail time, fled to Europe. He now lives in permanent exile in Paris, where he continues to make films.

7. MARLON BRANDO COMPOUND, 12900 Mulholland Drive

Brando had even worse trouble in this $4 million compound, which is located behind the same security gate as Nicholson's. On May 16, 1990, Brando's son Christian shot and killed Dag Drollet, the lover of Brando's daughter's. Christian later pleaded guilty to a charge of voluntary manslaughter and received a 10-year prison sentence. (Neither Nicholson's nor Brando's homes are visible from the street.)

8. THE SUMMIT, 12000 Mulholland Drive

Another gated community, although not as posh as Beverly Park. Fred Roggin, Ed McMahon, Anita Pointer, and Eddie Van Halen and Valerie Bertenelli have homes here.

9. FORMER HOME OF RICK JAMES, 8115 Mulholland Terrace (just south of Mulholland Drive and west of Laurel Canyon Boulevard)

In 1991 Grammy Award-winning singer Rick James, best known for his song "Super Freak," and the mother of his son, Tanya Anne Hijazi, were charged with imprisoning and torturing a 24-year-old woman at this house. Police charged that James met the woman at a party, offered to put her up at his house, and then threatened to kill her if she left. James allegedly tied her up, forced the victim to orally copulate Hijazi, and burned her with a crack cocaine pipe. James, a recovering cocaine addict, beat that rap but was convicted in 1993 of a separate charge of assaulting and imprisoning another woman in another incident at what is now the Argyle Club on the Sunset Strip. James spent three years at the Folsom State Prison for that incident.

10. SO-CALLED "HOUDINI ESTATE," 2398 Laurel Canyon Boulevard

Just off the map, about 7/10 of a mile south of Mulholland Drive, are the ruins of an estate that several books on Hollywood identify as once belonging to Harry Houdini. About all that is left of the estate are the servants' quarters, steps which led to an Italian villa once standing on the site, and a bridge that seemed to once connect the villa with the houses located across the street on Laurel Canyon Boulevard.

Since Houdini once vowed to return from the dead, psychics still hold seances on the property, and legends persist that two ghosts—Houdini's plus the ghost of a mysterious woman dressed in green lingerie—haunt the estate. Houdini worked on several silent films in Hollywood in 1919, but a leading Houdini expert, Manny Weltman, insists that Houdini never leased or owned the property, and that during his Hollywood stay he either stayed at a fellow magician's home or in a studio bungalow. Unfortunately, title searches of the property do not reveal who owned the estate before 1922. To protect itself against charges of false advertising, a real estate company that tried to sell the property recently advertised it as the "estate known as Harry Houdini's."

11. FORMER HOME OF "JEOPARDY!" HOST ALEX TREBEK, 7966 Mulholland Drive

12. THE CHEMOSPHERE, 7776 Torreyson Drive (one block north of Mulholland Drive)

This is one of the most extraordinary houses in Southern California—if not the world. Shaped like an eight-sided flying saucer (and sometimes mistaken for one, particularly at night), the Chemosphere sits atop a single concrete post several hundred feet above Torreyson Drive. Brian DePalma used it in his 1984 film *Body Double* as the house where down-on-his-luck actor Craig Wasson (playing Jack Scully) becomes a pawn in a bizarre murder.

To get to the house, the occupants have to either climb more than 100 steps or take a cable car from the garage, which is on the street level, to the house's front door. The house was designed by the famed architect John Lautner, who also designed the house in *Diamonds are Forever* that James Bond rescued Willard Whyte from, after disposing of his bathing suit-clad bodyguards, Bambi and Thumper. Lautner also designed a house down the street at 7436 Mulholland that Mel Gibson brought down from its pedestal in *Lethal Weapon 2* (see next page).

The best views of the Chemosphere are from the corner of Torreyson Drive and Flynn Ranch Road or from across the street at 7777 Torreyson Drive.

13. ERROL FLYNN'S "MULHOLLAND HOUSE," 3100 Torreyson Place

Flynn threw wild parties here and installed one-way mirrors so he and his friends could watch his houseguests making love. The house was later owned by

Richard Dreyfuss, as well as Rick Nelson, who was the last person to live in the house before it was torn down. The property—sans house—was sold to the president of New York Seltzer for $4 million.

14. "LETHAL WEAPON 2" FILMING SITE, 7436 Mulholland Drive

In the movie *Lethal Weapon 2*, Mel Gibson tied the pedestal of this house, designed by John Lautner, to a pickup truck, and brought the house down by driving away. Of course, the house was not really destroyed. The producers built two exact duplicates of the house—one on Stage 1 at Burbank Studios; the other in Newhall, 20 miles north of Los Angeles, and destroyed those instead. It was the house in Newhall which plummeted to the bottom of the hill. In the movie the house was the residence of the evil ambassador of South Africa.

15. HOUSE REPORTED TO BE ARSENIO HALL'S, 7430 Pyramid Place

Arsenio has denied published reports that he bought this historic estate, once owned by Rudy Vallee, even though the title is in the name of his management company and the *Los Angeles Times* has identified him as being the owner. He has also denied knowledge of construction of a monstrous tennis court on the grounds, even after more than 100 of his neighbors, including actors Martin Landau and Robert Carradine, successfully petitioned the City Board of Zoning Appeals to stop the construction. In any event, the house, north of Mulholland, is not visible from the street.

John Lautner's "Flying Saucer" house in the Hollywood Hills.

OTHER CELEBRITIES WHO LIVE ON MUL-
HOLLAND DRIVE: Shaun Cassidy, Maryam D'Abo,
Bridget Fonda, Richard Grieco, Robin Leach, Julian
Lennon, Rob Lowe, and Harry Dean Stanton. Ernest
Borgnine, Wilt Chamberlain, Michael Dorn, Farrah
Fawcett, Anthony Gear, and Harry Hamlin own homes just
off Mulholland.

A number of celebrities also live in the Hollywood
Hills nearby: Dan Aykroyd, Justine Bateman, "Downtown
Julie" Brown, George Clooney, Morgan Fairchild, Valeria
Golino, Sally Kellerman, Greg Kinnear, Dinah Manoff,
Melanie Mayron, Joni Mitchell, Brian Robbins and Holly
Robinson, Gena Rowlands, Ione Skye, Susan Sullivan, Lea
Thompson and Daphne Zuniga. Robert Hays, Michael
Nader, Paul Rieser, Susan Ruttan and Stevie Wonder own
property on or just off Nichols Canyon.

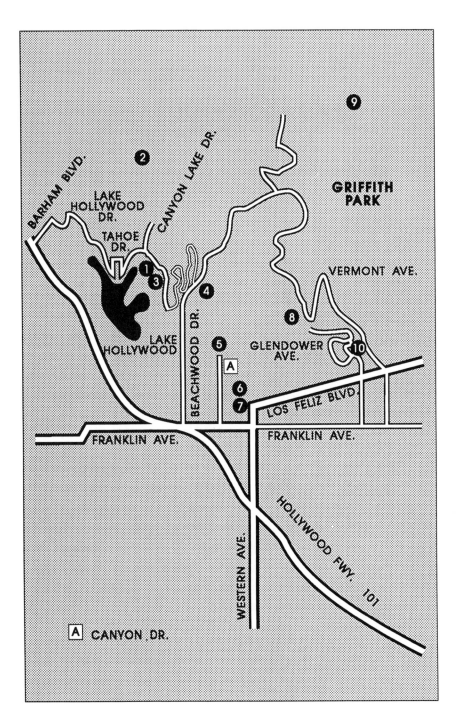

MAP 26   HOLLYWOODLAND & LOS FELIZ

HOLLYWOODLAND
AND LOS FELIZ

1. CASTILLO DEL LAGO, 6342 Mulholland Highway
(corner of Canyon Lake Drive)

Madonna lived in this nine-story-tall, 32-room, Spanish-style colonial mansion; purchasing it in 1993 for $5 million and selling it three years later for roughly the same price. While living there she horrified neighbors by painting it deep red with alternating red and yellow horizontal stripes over the compound's retaining wall and bell tower. The odd color scheme only added to the home's colorful history. In past years it had reportedly been used as a bordello and gambling den.

According to Charles Lockwood's *The Guide to Hollywood and Beverly Hills*, the castle was used by mobster Bugsy Siegel in the 1930s and "fit Bugsy's security needs perfectly—or so he thought. The only entrance was through a courtyard near the bottom of the house at the end of a long, narrow, winding driveway. The police would never attack the house from this approach. Because of the house's unobstructed views, Bugsy's strong-armed men thought that they could see the police coming from all other directions. But they were wrong. One night the police stormed Castillo del Lago from a neighboring house, and Bugsy's gambling-den days were over, at least for a while."

The best place to view the castle is from the hiking trail which runs along its side. (Incidentally, it is possible to hike from this castle to Wolf's Lair, a historic chateau described below. The trail, which is about half a mile long, provides the best views of Lake Hollywood, which was featured in both *Chinatown* and *Earthquake*. In *Earthquake,* the reservoir's dam collapsed, and the ensuing flood swept away all the people and buildings in its path.)

2. HOLLYWOOD SIGN, atop Mt. Lee

The Hollywood Sign, which is probably more recognizable worldwide than the Statue of Liberty or the White House, is actually a giant billboard with letters over fifty feet high and thirty feet wide. It was originally constructed in 1923 as "Hollywoodland" to advertise homes sold by the Hollywoodland Realty Company (still in existence in Beachwood Canyon), and when the last four letters of "Hollywoodland" fell off, the sign became a symbol of the entertainment industry itself.

Until recently, it was possible to hike to the sign from Mulholland Highway, which provides close-up views. However, a gate has since been erected to discourage vandals and jumps by the potentially suicidal.

3. WOLF'S LAIR, 2869 Durand Drive

Efrem Zimbalist, Jr., and Doris Day are former tenants of this intriguing chateau, situated at the end of the hiking trail alongside Castillo del Lago. The house was featured in the 1978 film *Return from Witch Mountain*, starring Bette Davis. Its original owner, Milton Wolf, a developer who designed the fairy tale-looking turrets, towers, and ramparts, died at the dining room table, leading to tales that this is one of L.A.'s many haunted houses.

Madonna's former home.

What appears to be a castle at 2818 Hollyridge Drive (at the corner of Pelham) is actually a false front to a conventional hillside home. Down the street, though, at 3030 Hollyridge Drive, is a real castle that can be seen from the street.

**4. "INVASION OF THE BODY SNATCHERS"
CHASE SITE**, corner Belden and Beachwood Drives

While some of the most memorable scenes in the original *Invasion of the Body Snatchers* were filmed in the town square of Sierra Madre, a small community just northeast of Pasadena (it was there that Kevin McCarthy and Dana Wynter hid from the pod people), the scenes of their escape were filmed at the corner of Beachwood and Belden Drives. The couple ran eastward up the hill on Belden Drive, and then up a flight of 148 steps actually located one block north of that intersection, at the corner of Beachwood and Woodshire Drives.

The area is one of the most intriguing in Hollywood, and do not be surprised if you see famous faces in the Beachwood Market at 2701 Belden Drive or the Village Coffee Shop two doors away.

5. BRONSON CAVES (at the end of Canyon Drive)

The Klingon prison camp in *Star Trek VI;* the Bat Cave in both the TV series "Batman" and the first feature film of the same name; the jungle island in the original *King Kong;* the ambush of the Lone Rangers, and the nursing back to health of "The Lone Ranger" by Tonto in the 1949 debut of the ABC western of that name; and numerous gunfights on "Gunsmoke," "Bonanza," and "Have Gun, Will Travel," were all filmed here. The caves are considered part of Griffith Park, but are not reachable through the park's main entrance. To see the caves, take Canyon Drive north until it ends, and hike a quarter of a mile up the trail to the right of the last parking lot.

6. NICOLAS CAGE'S CASTLE, 5647 Tryon Road

Cage paid $1.5 million in 1990 for this 5,367-square-foot castle which overlooks downtown L.A. The actor, who won an Academy Award for his role in *Leaving Las Vegas*, also owns a castle in Ireland, a Victorian house in San Francisco, a $3.5-million oceanfront home in Malibu, and, believe it or not, an apartment near Skid Row in downtown Los Angeles "so I can pretend I'm living incognito in some South American country."

7. AMERICAN FILM INSTITUTE, 2021 N. Western Avenue (north of Franklin Avenue), (213) 856-7600

Established in 1967, the American Film Institute is a prestigious nonprofit national arts organization devoted to preserving film and encouraging new talent. Its Center for Advanced Film and Television Studies offers specialized postgraduate training in producing, directing, screenwriting, cinematography and production design. Seminars and workshops are led by some of the top figures in the entertainment industry.

8. GRIFFITH PARK OBSERVATORY, 2800 E. Observatory Road, (213) 664-1191

Griffith Park—which is the largest urban park in the United States—is sometimes referred to as an unofficial Hollywood back lot since so many productions are filmed there. Says the park's film coordinator: "When companies need green space or a road that doesn't have buildings on it, they come here." Blast-off scenes in *The Rocketeer*, the final fight scenes in *Rebel Without a Cause*, and the opening scenes of *The Terminator*, in which Arnold Schwarzenegger traveled back in time, were filmed at the park observatory. A bust of James Dean stands on the planetarium's west front lawn.

The Griffith Park Observatory.

9. LOS ANGELES ZOO, 5333 Zoo Drive, (213) 666-4090
        Seen in opening credits of the 1977-84 ABC sitcom "Three's Company."

10. ENNIS-BROWN HOUSE, 2655 Glendower Avenue
        In the 1991 feature *Grand Canyon*, Steve Martin, who played the obnoxious producer Davis, lived in this architecturally historic house, which was designed by Frank Lloyd Wright to resemble a Mayan temple. Martin's character was based on a real-life producer, Joel Silver, who, interestingly enough, happens to own two

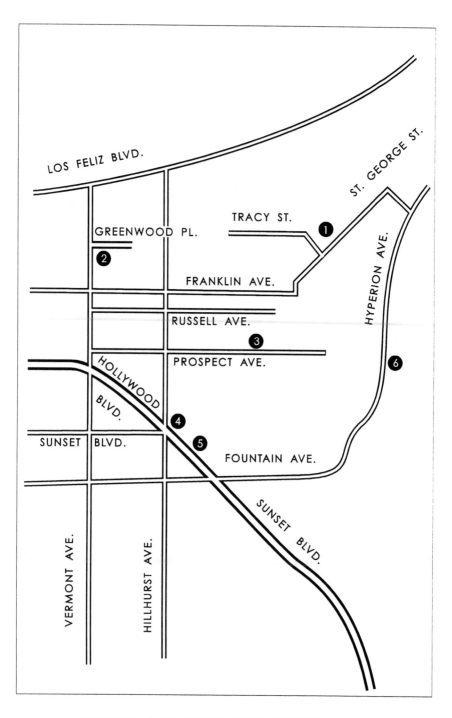

MAP 27   LOS FELIZ AND SILVER LAKE

houses designed by Wright—one in South Carolina, the other a similarly-designed Mayan temple at 8161 Hollywood Boulevard, just north of the Sunset Strip.

The Ennis-Brown House was also featured in *Blade Runner* (the exterior served as Harrison Ford's home), *Karate Kid III,* and *Black Rain.* Tours of the Ennis-Brown House are conducted on the second Saturdays of January, March, May, July, September and November. For tour information call (213) 660-0607.

---

1. JOHN MARSHALL HIGH SCHOOL, 3939 Tracy Street

This high school was Rydell High School in *Grease,* Dason High in *Rebel Without a Cause,* Hemery High in the feature film *Buffy the Vampire Slayer,* and Jefferson High in the 1963-65 NBC drama "Mr. Novak."

Marshall alumni include actors Leonard DiCaprio and Julie Newmar. Heidi Fleiss was a Marshall dropout.

2. "MELROSE PLACE" APARTMENT BUILDING, 4616 Greenwood Place

Set designers added foliage to transform this dumpy-looking apartment into the modern building seen on the campy Fox-TV show. Novelist Raymond Chandler lived here in the early 1930s.

3. ABC TELEVISION CENTER, 4151 Prospect Avenue

The facility was originally built in 1912 by Vitagraph, one of the pioneer film companies, and was later bought by Warner Bros. in 1925. Warner turned the lot into a studio annex. In 1947 the facility was purchased by the just-created ABC Television Network. Since then the broadcasting facility has been used to produce ABC network shows and is the home of KABC-TV (channel 7), the Los Angeles-owned and operated station of Capitol Cities/ABC Inc. The studio does not offer a public tour, but it is possible to see the taping of some ABC shows. For ticket information, call the ABC Show Ticket Hotline, (310) 520-1ABC, or write to ABC Guest Services, 4151 Prospect Avenue, Los Angeles, CA 90027.

4. SITE OF "BABYLON," 4500 Sunset Boulevard
Although long gone, the largest outdoors movie set ever built—the city of Babylon built for D. W. Griffith's 1916 silent film classic *Intolerance*—stood at this site for years.

5. KCET, 4401 Sunset Boulevard
One of the oldest continually used studios in Hollywood. Allied Artists, Monogram Pictures, and other long forgotten studios have made mostly "B" movies here ever since 1912. Since 1971 the site has been occupied by KCET, Southern California's public television station (channel 28). In *L.A. Story*, KCET doubled as KYOY, where Steve Martin played a daffy television weatherman. Free one-hour tours are offered on Tuesdays and Thursdays.

6. ONE-TIME SITE OF WALT DISNEY'S FIRST OFFICIAL STUDIO, 2701-39 Hyperion Avenue
A Mayfair Food Market now occupies the land where *Snow White and the Seven Dwarfs* was produced as the first feature-length animated film. The site was declared a historic cultural monument by the city of Los Angeles in 1976.

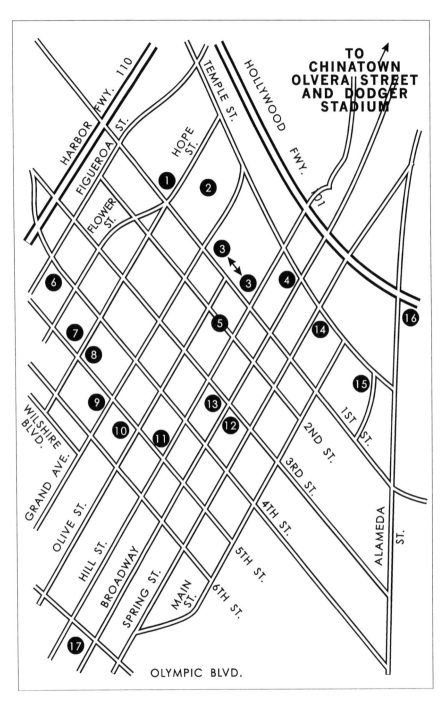

MAP 28 DOWNTOWN

DOWNTOWN

1. DEPARTMENT OF WATER AND POWER, 111 N. Hope Street

The exterior of the DWP building was used as the 14th Precinct in "Cagney and Lacey," and Tacoma police headquarters in *Three Fugitives*. The garage parking lot was used for shoot-out and chase scenes in *The Terminator*.

2. DOROTHY CHANDLER PAVILION, 135 N. Grand Avenue, (213) 972-7211

The marble and black-glass Pavilion is the winter home of the Los Angeles Philharmonic and the site of most of the annual Academy Award presentations since 1969. The Pavilion seats 3,000, but since there are 5,000 members of the Academy of Motion Picture Arts and Sciences and most members bring guests to the ceremonies, the Academy tries to make its membership happy by holding ceremonies every third or fourth year at the larger (6,000-seat) Shrine Auditorium (see page 207), even though the cost of feeding its members and accommodating the world press is considerably higher at the Shrine.

3. LOS ANGELES COUNTY COURTHOUSE, 111 N. Hill Street

4. CRIMINAL COURTS BUILDING, 210 W. Temple Street (at Broadway)

Site of O. J. Simpson's 1995 acquittal of double murder charges.

5. SECOND STREET TUNNEL (between Hill and Figueroa Streets)

Used frequently in movie chase scenes—including *The Terminator, Demolition Man* and *Con Air.* For the *Independence Day* alien attack, the filmmakers staged a huge traffic jam involving over 300 cars, trucks and buses. Wil Smith's girlfriend, played by Vivica A. Fox, narrowly escaped the fireball consuming downtown Los Angeles by kicking open a tunnel door, dragging her son and dog with her. In *Set It Off,* the story of young black women who robbed banks for revenge against personal injustices, Fox and her partners-in-crime, Jada Pinkett and Queen Latifah, were trapped in the tunnel by the LAPD.

6. WESTIN BONAVENTURE, 404 S. Figueroa Street, (213) 624-1000

In the 1993 feature *In The Line of Fire,* Clint Eastwood, playing an aging Secret Service agent assigned to protect the president, thwarted John Malkovich's assassination attempt here. The same glass elevator used for the climactic scene, in which Malkovich held Eastwood hostage, was also featured in one of the more memorable scenes in *True Lies.* In that movie, Arnold Schwarzenegger, riding a horse he "borrowed" from a policeman, pursued a terrorist by galloping through the Bonaventure lobby, and continuing the pursuit on the elevator.

Assassins returned to the Bonaventure for the John Badham-directed *Nick of Time,* this time for a plot against a liberal governor of California who was campaigning for re-election. Johnny Depp played a mild-mannered accountant who was sucked into the plot when Christopher Walken and Roma Maffia kidnapped his daughter and threatened to kill her unless Depp killed the governor. Bonaventure employees played an heroic role in thwarting that plot.

The futuristic-looking Bonaventure has also been featured in *Strange Days, My Fellow Americans, Blue Thunder, Ruthless People, Mr. Mom, Virtuosity, The Poseidon Adventure,* and *Lethal Weapon 2.* In a scene for *Rainman* filmed by the hotel's pool, Tom Cruise rejected a $250,000 bribe to return his autistic brother to an Ohio mental institution. The frenetic shoot-out in *Heat* was filmed just outside the Bonaventure, at the corner of Fourth and Flower Streets. The hotel's BonaVista Lounge on the 35th floor was also where the daffy waitresses in the 1980s sitcom "It's a Living" worked.

7. "L.A. LAW" BUILDING, 444 S. Flower Street

While this building is best known as the building seen in TV's "L.A. Law," its offices have also been used for *Baby Boom, Black Rain, Beverly Hills Cop II,* and *Gotcha!,* where it served as CIA headquarters. The building was also used as the exterior of the bank Robert De Niro and Val Kilmer robbed in *Heat.*

8. FIRST INTERSTATE BANK BUILDING, 633 W. 5th Street

Fittingly, this 60-story skyscraper—the tallest building on the west coast—was where the aliens in *Independence Day* struck first, wiping out flaky Angelinos who tried to stage a welcoming party on the building's rooftop.

In the less successful *Life Stinks*, Mel Brooks had his offices here. Brooks played a developer who accepted a rival's challenge to try to survive for one month on Skid Row.

9. REGAL BILTMORE HOTEL, 506 S. Grand Street (at Fifth Street), (213) 624-1011; in California (800) 252-0175

Since it opened in 1923, the Biltmore has hosted kings, presidents, Hollywood celebrities and virtually every major league baseball team. In 1960 John F. Kennedy set up the official headquarters for the Democratic National Convention in the Music Room (now the lobby), and it was here that JFK and his brother Bobby decided on Lyndon Baines Johnson as JFK's running mate. A few years later, the Beatles, who had been mobbed by fans during their first U.S. tour, secretly helicoptered to the hotel's rooftop and hid at the Biltmore until moving to another location.

Over the last 20 years at least 300 feature films, television programs, and commercials have been filmed at the hotel. In perhaps its most memorable appearance, Eddie Murphy conned his way into the hotel in *Beverly Hills Cop*. Murphy later returned to the Biltmore to confront a potential research donor (James Coburn) in *The Nutty Professor*. Ben Kingsley and his crew of alien-hunters chose the hotel as command central in *Species*. The Crystal Ballroom served as the setting for the bookie joint in *The Sting*, the fight arena in *Rocky III*, the prom scene in *Pretty in Pink,* the banquet scene in *Alien Nation*, the singing scenes in *The Fabulous Baker Boys*, and the slime scenes in *Ghostbusters*. *Vertigo* used the 11 flights of ornate, wrought-iron back stairs to create its dizzying scenes; and scenes from *Bugsy* and *The Fan* were filmed at the Biltmore Health Club. The hotel's other credits include *Independence Da*y, *Romy and Michele's High School Reunion, True Lies, The American President, My Fellow Americans, Mother*, and *In The Line of Fire* (where it appeared as the hotel in Denver where Clint Eastwood and Rene Russo stayed.)

The Biltmore was also the setting of eight early Academy Award ceremonies: in 1931, 1935 through 1939, and 1941 and 1942. Actors Delta Burke and Gerald McRaney got married here in 1989.

10. GAS COMPANY TOWER, 555 Fifth Street (at Grand Street)

Directly across the street from the Biltmore is the 54-story office building featured in the opening scenes of *Speed.* Keanu Reeves and Jeff Daniels rescued office workers trapped in a collapsing elevator.

11. TITLE GUARANTEE AND TRUST BUILDING, 411 W. Fifth Street (at Hill Street, across from Pershing Square)

The exterior of this Art Deco building was depicted as the *Los Angeles Tribune* in the 1977-82 CBS drama "Lou Grant." Today the Spanish-language newspaper *La Opinion* has offices here.

12. BRADBURY BUILDING, 304 S. Broadway (at 3rd Street)

This historic building has been the setting of several television and movie private eye melodramas, including *Chinatown.* In *Blade Runner*, Harrison Ford searched for androids here. The Bradbury also served as Jack Nicholson's publishing office in *Wolf,* Christian

Slater's law office in *Murder in the First,* and Dean Stockwell's detective office in *Mr. Wrong.*

Sam Hall Kaplan, L.A.'s premier architectural critic, writes: "With its magical interior court bathed in light filtered through a glass roof and ornate ironwork and reflected off glazed yellow brick walls, the 1893 structure is one of the city's architectural treasures."

(Note: In this part of town, bring plenty of quarters to fend off the panhandlers.)

13. MILLION DOLLAR THEATER, 307 S. Broadway

This architecturally intriguing movie palace was built by showman Sid Grauman in 1917, five years before he built the Egyptian Theater in Hollywood and ten years before he built the Chinese Theater.

14. CITY HALL, 200 N. Spring Street

"City Hall," writes *Los Angeles Times* researcher Cecilia Rasmussen, "has starred in more movies and television series than most Hollywood actors." Perhaps best known as the *Daily Planet* in the popular 1950s television series "Superman," City Hall, inside and out, has been seen in *It Seems Like Old Times, 48 Hours, Another 48 Hours, Die Hard II, Dragnet,* and *Ricochet.* "Although it was destroyed by Martians in *War of the Worlds,*" Rasmussen notes, "it somehow survived to portray the U.S. Capitol in 'The Jimmy Hoffa Story' and the Vatican in 'The Thorn Birds' . . . You might have caught a glimpse of City Hall in the series 'Kojak,' 'Cagney and Lacey,' 'The Rockford Files,' 'Matlock,' 'Hill Street Blues,' 'L.A. Law,' 'Equal Justice,' 'The Trials of Rosie O'Neill,' and 'The Big One: The Great Los Angeles Earthquake.'"

Los Angeles' City Hall.

The Shrine Auditorium.

204

15. PARKER CENTER, 150 N. Los Angeles Street

Headquarters for the Los Angeles Police Department. Seen in numerous television cop shows, most notably "Dragnet."

16. UNION STATION, 800 N. Alameda Street, (213) 683-6987

Union Station has been featured in *Grand Canyon, Blade Runner, Guilty by Suspicion, Bugsy, The Way We Were, Dear God, Nick of Time, Species,* several television series, and of course, the 1950 movie *Union Station* starring William Holden. (Although there is a brief establishing shot of the station in *Silver Streak,* that movie was mostly filmed in Canada. The film required several stunts, and the station's management company does not grant filming permission to filmmakers who use on-site stunt work.)

17. HERALD EXAMINER BUILDING, 1111 S. Broadway

After the *Los Angeles Herald Examiner* went out of business in 1989, a location company moved in, and the building is now used exclusively as a location site for television shows and movies. The building itself is one of Los Angeles' most intriguing architectural landmarks. It was designed by Julia Morgan, the pioneering architect whose design so pleased William Randolph Hearst that he commissioned her to build his oceanside mansion in Santa Monica and his castle at San Simeon.

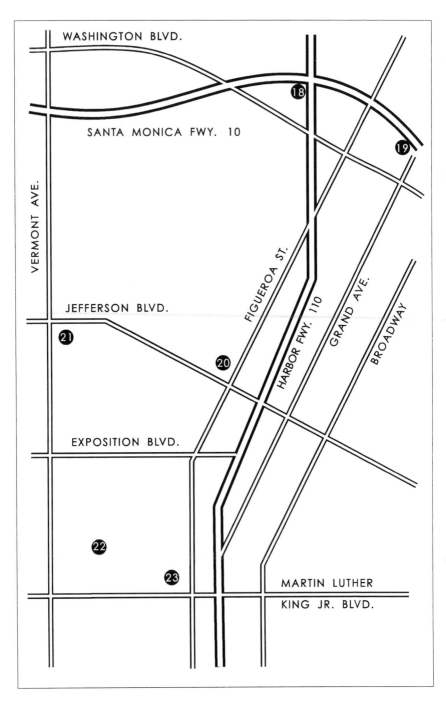

MAP 29 DOWNTOWN

18. "CHIPs" HEADQUARTERS, 777 W. Washington Boulevard

The exterior of the Central Los Angeles office of the California Highway Patrol was used in the 1977-1983 NBC action series "CHIPs."

19. OLYMPIC AUDITORIUM, 1801 S. Grand Avenue (south of 10 and east of 110)

Many of Sylvester Stallone's boxing scenes in *Rocky* were filmed here.

20. SHRINE AUDITORIUM, 649 W. Jefferson Boulevard

The largest theater in the United States, the Shrine has been the site of ceremonies for the Academy Awards, the Grammys, the American Music Awards, and the MTV Awards. In the original *King Kong,* the gorilla was paraded in front of the auditorium and broke away from his chains. In *Naked Gun 33 1/3*, Leslie Nielsen disrupted an Academy Awards ceremony while thwarting a terrorist plot. Goldie Hawn appeared from under a stage in *Foul Play*, and extras danced bare-chested for Oliver Stone during a concert filmed for his movie *The Doors*. The Shrine was also where Michael Jackson's hair caught on fire during the filming of a Pepsi commercial.

21. USC SCHOOL OF CINEMA AND TELEVISION, 850 W. 34 Street (by Jefferson Boulevard and McClintock Avenue)

USC, along with New York University, is widely considered to be the premier film school in the country. Its film school is modeled after a Hollywood studio, and includes sound stages, screening rooms, classrooms and administrative offices. Alumni in the arts include *Star*

Wars creator George Lucas; directors Ron Howard (who did not graduate), Robert Zemeckis, John Singleton, Phillip Joanou, and Michael Lehmann; and screenwriter Amanda Silver.

Over 30 movies have been filmed on campus, including *Forrest Gump* (where it doubled for the University of Alabama), *The Graduate* (where it portrayed Berkeley), *The Paper Chase* (Harvard), *Blue Chips*, *Rising Sun*, *Mr. Baseball*, *Soul Man*, and the 1939 classic *The Hunchback of Notre Dame,* which featured Notre Dame's Quasimado in the library's bell tower.

22. LOS ANGELES MEMORIAL COLISEUM, 3911 S. Figueroa Street

The Coliseum is the only arena that has hosted two Olympic games (1932 and 1984), two Super Bowls (1967 and 1972), a World Series (1959), and a Papal visit (Pope John Paul II in 1987). The opening and closing scenes of *The Last Boy Scout* were filmed here, as were the climactic scenes in *Black Sunday* and the gladiatorial basketball scenes in *Escape from L.A.* The Coliseum now offers group guided tours; call (213) 748-6136, extension 399, for information.

23. LOS ANGELES MEMORIAL SPORTS ARENA, 3939 S. Figueroa Street

Built in 1959, the Sports Arena hosts over 200 events each year, including the games of the NBA's Los Angeles Clippers and USC's men's and women's basketball teams. In 1960 John F. Kennedy was nominated for the presidency at the Democratic National Convention held here. Some of the fight scenes in *Rocky* were filmed at the Sports Arena.

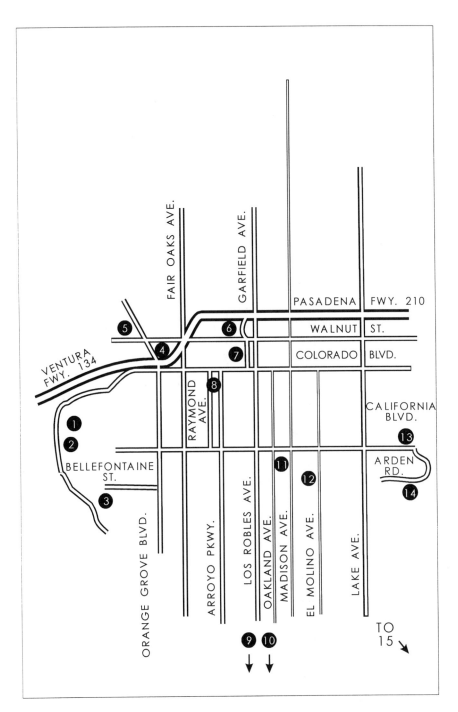

MAP 30 PASADENA

PASADENA

1. THE INCORRECTLY IDENTIFIED "BATMAN MANSION," 160 S. San Rafael Avenue (south of Colorado Avenue)

This extraordinary three-story Tudor mansion has been cited in other tour books as the house used as the Wayne Manor in the 1960s television series "Batman." However, Tonie Carnes, a researcher for the Pasadena Historical Society, discovered that the real Bat House was actually down the street a few blocks at 380 S. San Rafael Avenue. 160 S. San Rafael Avenue is not without its significance, though; it was used as a mansion in *Mobsters,* and as Sylvester Stallone's home in *Rocky V.*

2. THE REAL "BATMAN MANSION," 380 S. San Rafael Avenue

Unfortunately, the real Bat Mansion is not visible from the street. Neighbors say that the frequent filming at this mansion has sometimes created a carnival-like atmosphere on the street. The house, known to location scouts as Dr. Oh's (the doctor owns it), also served as Kenneth Branaugh's home in *Dead Again.*

3. MAYFIELD SENIOR SCHOOL, 500 Bellafontaine Street

One of Pasadena's most popular location sites (mostly for television series, movies of the week, soap operas and commercials), this private all-girls Catholic school was seen in *The Lost World, The Shadow, Sneakers, Devil in a Blue Dress,* and *Newsies.* Behind the school, on Bellafontaine Terrace, is the house seen in the TV sitcom "Valerie" starring Valerie Harper, in 1986. When Harper was replaced by Sandy Duncan the following year, the program became "Valerie's Family," and then "The Hogan Family," which aired on NBC, and then CBS, until 1990.

4. FENYES MANSION, 470 W. Walnut Street (corner of Orange Grove), (818) 577-1660

Now the permanent home of the Pasadena Historical Society, this mansion was one of two mansions used in Hal Ashby's 1979 feature *Being There.* (The other was the Fenyes Mansion at 430 Madeline Avenue—now the home of the Red Cross.) In the movie, Peter Sellers played the caretaker whose ignorance was mistaken for profundity. Scenes from *Newsies* were also filmed there.

5. GAMBLE HOUSE, 4 Westmoreland Place (half a block north of the Fenyes Mansion, on a small, poorly marked side street just west of and reachable from Orange Grove)

In the *Back to the Future* movies, Christopher Lloyd ("Doc") lived in this house. The house, built in 1908 for David and Mary Gamble of Procter & Gamble, is an internationally recognized architectural landmark, a product of the turn-of-the-century Arts and Crafts movement. For tour hours, call (818) 793-3334.

6. PASADENA PUBLIC LIBRARY, 285 E. Walnut Street

The library was Mara Wilson's hangout in *Matilda* and the San Francisco library in which Goldie Hawn worked in *Foul Play.* Jeff Daniels researched insects here in *Arachnophobia.*

7. PASADENA CITY HALL, 100 N. Garfield Avenue

Used by the producers of the first two *Beverly Hills Cop* movies as the exterior of Beverly Hills City Hall. (Filming permits cost less in Pasadena than in Beverly Hills.) City Hall was also a French castle in *Patton* and a San Francisco courthouse in *Murder in the First.* The larger courtyard served as the site of Napa Valley's annual harvest festival and parade in *A Walk in the Clouds.*

The Gamble House.

8. CASTLE GREEN APARTMENTS, 99 S. Raymond Avenue (corner of Green Street)

One of Pasadena's premier resort hotels before the turn of the century, the Castle Green is a popular location site because of its unusual Middle Eastern architecture. The outside of the building was used as the Hotel Nacional de Cuba in *Bugsy*, as a Russian consular office in San Francisco in *Sneakers*, and as a restaurant in *The Marrying Man*. It was also where "the sting" took place in *The Sting*.

Public tours are conducted twice a year—usually in April and in December—by Pasadena Heritage and the residents of the Castle Green. For further information call the Castle Green at (818) 793-0359.

9. "BENSON MANSION," 1365 S. Oakland Avenue

The exterior of this house was used as the Governor's mansion on the popular sitcom "Benson," which aired on ABC from 1979 to 1986.

10. "BEVERLY HILLBILLIES" MOVIE HOUSE, 1284 S. Oakland Avenue

Used for the exterior shots of the Clampett residence in *The Beverly Hillbillies* movie. Interior scenes were filmed in four different mansions in Beverly Hills.

11. "DENNIS THE MENACE" HOUSE, 830 S. Madison Avenue

This was the house seen in the 1959-63 CBS sitcom "Dennis the Menace," starring Jay North.

12. "FATHER OF THE BRIDE" HOUSE, 843 S. El Molino Avenue

Although the 1991 remake of *Father of the Bride* identified Steve Martin and Diane Keaton's residence as being located in San Marino, the house was actually located in Pasadena, a few blocks north of San Marino (which discourages filmmaking by making their permits more expensive). The producers considered the house to be almost a character in the story. They looked for a house in an old-fashioned, idealized community—and considered this white clapboard residence perfect.

13. CALIFORNIA INSTITUTE OF TECHNOLOGY, 1201 E. California Boulevard (between Hill and Wilson Avenues)

Caltech would rather be known for its inventions (the seismograph and Richter scale); its scientific discoveries (its labs discovered anti-matter, quasars, quarks, the nature of the chemical bond, and the left brain-right brain hemispheres); its illustrious faculty and alumni (over 21 Nobel Laureates); and its consistent ranking as one of the top research universities in the world. Of course, since it is so close to Hollywood, Caltech occasionally shows up on the silver screen. The Athenaeum—a faculty dining club originally conceived as a meeting place for scholars—appeared in both *Beverly Hills Cop* I and II. In the first film it was the private club Eddie Murphy conned his way into, resulting in a fight in which Murphy threw Jonathan Banks across a buffet table. In *Beverly Hills Cop II*, the Athenaeum was used again as the site of the movie's villain-infested Beverly Hills Shooting Club. Caltech exteriors were viewed in *Real Genius, The War of the Roses, Funny About Love*, and *The Witches of Eastwick.*

14. "THE CARRINGTON MANSION," 1145 Arden Road

This is not the house seen in the opening credits of "Dynasty" (that one is located in the San Francisco suburb of Woodside). It is, however, the one that was used for the garden and pool shots (including Joan Collins' famous fights with Linda Evans) and for close-up outdoor scenes with the actors. The 20,000-square-foot mansion, Arden Villa, has been a frequent filming site, dating back to the 1933 Marx Brothers' classic *Duck Soup*. According to Charles Morton, a former owner who still handles filming and corporate affair rentals at the mansion, Arden Villa has appeared in at least 200 productions since 1980, including four television movies about the Kennedys, "Nixon's Last Days," several episodes of "Hart to Hart," "Flamingo Road," Eddie Murphy's *The Distinguished Gentleman* and Charles Bronson's *Death Wish*. The house also served as the Knight Rider Foundation in the 1982-86 NBC adventure series "Knight Riders."

15. THE HUNTINGTON LIBRARY, ART COL-LECTIONS, AND BOTANICAL GARDENS, 1151 Oxford Road, San Marino, (818) 405-2141

This museum features 18th and 19th century British and French art, rare books and manuscripts, and 150 acres of botanical gardens. The Huntington Gallery was portrayed as Robert Redford's mansion in *Indecent Proposal*, and the grounds were also the site of the tented party in *The Nutty Professor* and Robert and Anna's wedding in "General Hospital." Other movies filmed on the grounds include *Beverly Hills Ninja, Coming to America, A Little Princess, Edwards and Hunt, MacArthur,* and *War and Remembrance*.

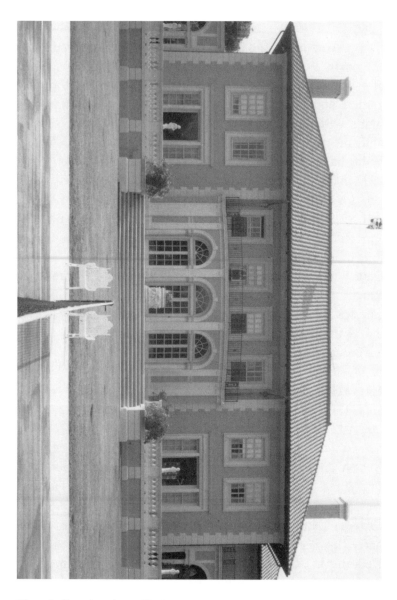

The oft-filmed Arden Villa in Pasadena, seen in the popular TV series "Dynasty."

JUST OFF THE MAP, in South Pasadena, are a number of homes filmed in movies and television series. The Philadelphia house that Ken Olin and Mel Harris supposedly lived in on "thirtysomething" was actually located at 1710 Bushnell Avenue in South Pasadena. Owner Donna Potts told a reporter that a location scout just came to the door one day before filming began and later offered a contract to the family. The house directly across the street—at 1711 Bushnell—was both the 1955 house where Lea Thompson and her family took in Michael J. Fox in *Back to the Future*, and Fox's home in *Teen Wolf*. In the *Back to the Future* series, 1711 served as Crispin Glover's home, 1705 as Elisabeth Shue's, and 1809 as Thomas Wilson's. 1621 and 1615 Bushnell were both used as Bill Cosby's home in *Ghost Dad*.

One block west, at 1632 Fletcher, is Patricia Wettig and Tim Busfield's house in "thirtysomething." Another block west of that is Milan Avenue, where Charles Grodin lived in *Beethoven* (at 1405). The house in the 1976-80 ABC series "Family" is on the 600 block of Milan.

In South Pasadena's historic business district is Carrows Restaurant (815 S. Fremont Avenue), where Linda Hamilton, playing Sarah Connor, waitressed in *The Terminator*. Down the street, at 1518 Mission Street, is L. L. Balk Hardware—the hardware store where Fox worked at in *Teen Wolf*. Around the corner from L. L. Balk is the Rialto Theater, at 1023 S. Fair Oaks Avenue. It was at the Rialto that Tim Robbins, playing a studio executive in Robert Altman's 1992 feature *The Player,* met Vincent D'Onofrio, who played the writer whom Robbins thought was sending him threatening postcards. In the movie Robbins killed D'Onofrio behind the theater.

Also off the map—in the western section of Pasadena (just north of the Gamble House and south of the

Rose Bowl)—is Brookside Park. In *High Anxiety*, Mel Brooks paid homage to Alfred Hitchcock's classic *The Birds* by filming a scene there in which he was drenched by bird droppings.

Between Pasadena and Glendale is the community of Eagle Rock, home of Occidental College. The college played California University in the TV series "Beverly Hills 90210."

The Walsh family home on "Beverly Hills 90210" is actually located at 1675 East Altadena Drive in Altadena, about four miles northeast of downtown Pasadena and a good forty minutes' drive from Beverly Hills.

The Queen Anne cottage seen in the television series "Fantasy Island" is located at the Los Angeles State and County Arboretum, at 301 N. Baldwin Avenue in Arcadia, no more than a ten-minute drive southeast of downtown Pasadena. The arboretum is a 127-acre botanical park which features exotic trees and shrubs arranged by their continent of origin. The opening sequence of "Fantasy Island" included stock footage of an airplane landing on the lake and Herve Villechaise's character, Tatoo, ringing the bell in the cottage tower, yelling "De plane, de plane." The producers actually only filmed a few episodes at the Arboretum, and then constructed a replica on the studio lot. The Arboretum has appeared in well over 200 television episodes and films, including eight Tarzan movies, *The African Queen, The Road to Singapore*, and other movies with jungle settings. For hours, call (213) 681-8411.

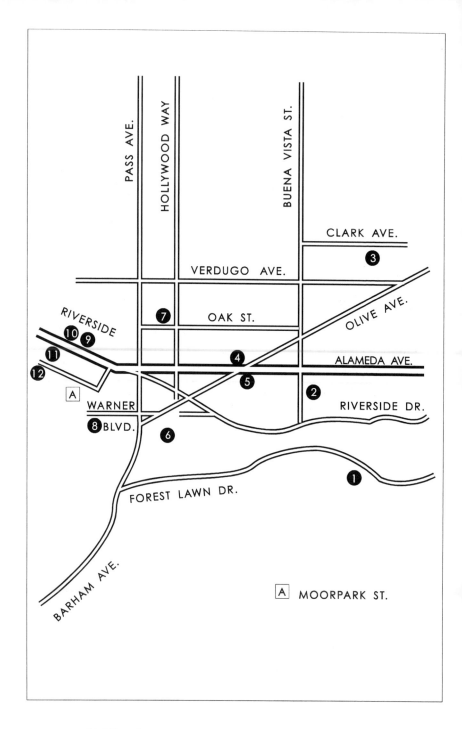

MAP 31   BURBANK AND TOLUCA LAKE

BURBANK AND TOLUCA LAKE

1. FOREST LAWN MEMORIAL PARK HOLLY-WOOD HILLS, 6300 Forest Lawn Drive

This huge cemetery is the final resting place of Lucille Ball, Bette Davis, Sammy Davis, Jr., Redd Fox, Andy Gibb, Buster Keaton, Stan Laurel, Liberace, Ozzie Nelson, Freddie Prinze, George Raft, Gene Roddenberry, and Jack Webb. Park maps are available at the front gates, but they do not show the locations of the stars' graves. A book published in 1989, *Permanent Californians: An Illustrated Guide to the Cemeteries of California* by Judi Culbertson and Tom Randall, does. That book also covers celebrity graves at Forest Lawn Glendale, 1712 S. Glendale Avenue, where many other luminaries are buried and where Ronald Reagan married Jane Wyman on January 27, 1940, at the Wee Kirk o' the Heather Church.

2. DISNEY STUDIOS, 500 S. Buena Vista Street

Since 1940, this has been the headquarters of Disney Studios, a company whose movies are loved by children—and whose tight-fisted business dealings are less loved by writers, producers and agents. In an article for *Vanity Fair*, journalist Peter J. Boyer called Disney "a place so reviled that even its architecture inspires nasty rumors, such as the apocryphal story that architect Michael Graves arranged the drainage system in the Disney headquarters building in such a way that the huge sculpted Seven Dwarfs atop the edifice would seem to be peeing on

Disney executives whenever it rained." Boyer also called Disney "a place so tough in its dealings with the outside, so rigidly demanding of its own people, that it has earned an unlovely nickname that will be hard to erase. They call it Mouschwitz."

Of course, those who run Disney know that most people will not care how they treat the people who work with or for them, and will more likely associate Disney with its wonderful fairy tale movies such as *Snow White and the Seven Dwarfs, The Little Mermaid, Beauty and the Beast, Alladin, 101 Dalmations*, and *The Lion King* as well as its famous television shows: "Zorro," "Dragnet," and "The Wonderful World of Disney." The studio, apparently not wishing to compete with Disneyland, does not offer a tour of its facilities.

The Disney administration building.

3. BURROUGHS HIGH SCHOOL, 1920 Clark Avenue

One of the high schools used in filming the Emmy Award-winning "The Wonder Years." Alumni include Debbie Reynolds, Ron Howard and Rene Russo. While promoting *Ransom*, directed by Howard and co-starring Russo, the actress repeatedly told reporters how she used to cheat off Howard during tests. Russo was a Burroughs dropout.

4. DICK CLARK PRODUCTIONS, 3003 W. Olive Avenue

These are the offices of Clark's production company, which produces the American Music Awards, the Golden Globe Awards, the Academy of Country Music Awards, "New Year's Rockin' Eve," movies made for television and game shows. No tours.

(Note: If you have ever wanted to take a side trip to beautiful downtown Burbank, just take Olive Avenue north. It has been revitalized since Johnny Carson joked about it in his monologues. The house featured in the ABC comedy-drama "The Wonder Years" is just northwest of downtown at 516 University Avenue.)

5. NBC STUDIOS, 3000 W. Alameda Avenue

NBC is the only television network which offers a tour of its studios. It is also possible to see a taping of "The Tonight Show" and other shows filmed at the studio. The studio's ticket counter opens at 8:00 A.M. and distributes tickets for shows that tape for that evening. Ticket requests are also honored by mail if you write to the studio with the name of the show and enclose a self-addressed stamped envelope. NBC's ticket information number is (818) 840-3537.

NBC Studios in Burbank.

An aerial view of Warner Bros.

6. WARNER BROS. STUDIOS, 4000 Warner Boulevard

Warner Bros., which has been headquarted here since 1929, offers a two-hour tour of its back lot and studio facilities. The tour, Warner spokespersons point out, "is not a charade created for mass audiences, but is, in fact, designed for small groups—no more than 12 persons—so that they may learn about the various components that go into the making of a film."

Since each tour guide is allowed to customize his or her own tour, and activity on the lot changes daily, no two tours are identical. However, all stop by the new Warner Bros. Museum and visit the back lot sets where hundreds of feature films and episodic television shows have been filmed over the years. Tourists are allowed to wander around some of these sets and take pictures, provided that they are not being used for upcoming productions. Seeing a television show or feature being filmed on the back lot is not guaranteed, but it is a common occurrence. No one under 10 is admitted. For prices and hours call (818) 954-1744.

7. WARNER BROS. RANCH FACILITIES, 3701 W. Oak Street

Behind the walls of this 40-acre back lot are sound stages and movie sets used in countless movies. The streets include the facade of "Murphy Brown"'s townhouse, the houses from "Bewitched," "I Dream of Jeannie," and "The Partridge Family," Danny Glover's house in *Lethal Weapon 2*, and Garp's house in *The World According to Garp*. The back lot is only sometimes shown during the Warner Bros. tour and is not otherwise open to the public.

8. "SCARECROW AND MRS. KING" HOUSE, 4247 Warner Boulevard

The exterior of this Cape Cod was used as Kate Jackson and Beverly Garland's home in the 1983-87 CBS adventure series "Scarecrow and Mrs. King."

9. PATY'S RESTAURANT, 10001 Riverside Drive, (818) 760-9164

A good spot to catch a glimpse of celebrities who work at nearby studios.

10. LONGTIME HOME OF BOB HOPE, 10346 Moorpark Street

The comedian bought this white-brick, 15-room house in 1940.

CELEBRITIES WHO LIVE IN TOLUCA LAKE: Andy Garcia, Charles Haid, Garry Marshall, Park Overall, Markie Post, John Ratzenberger, Alan Thicke, Denzel Washington, Jonathan Winters, and Joanne Worley. Former residents include Bing Crosby, Andy Griffith and Jerry Van Dyke (all of whom lived at 10050 Camarillo Street), W. C. Fields, William Holden, Moe Howard, Al Jolson, Frank Sinatra, and Henry Winkler.

According to *Letters from Amelia*, famed aviator Amelia Earhart bought the house at the very end of Valley Spring Lane, across from Lakeside Country Club, in 1935, two years before she mysteriously disappeared while trying to fly around the world.

Filming on the Universal Studios backlot.

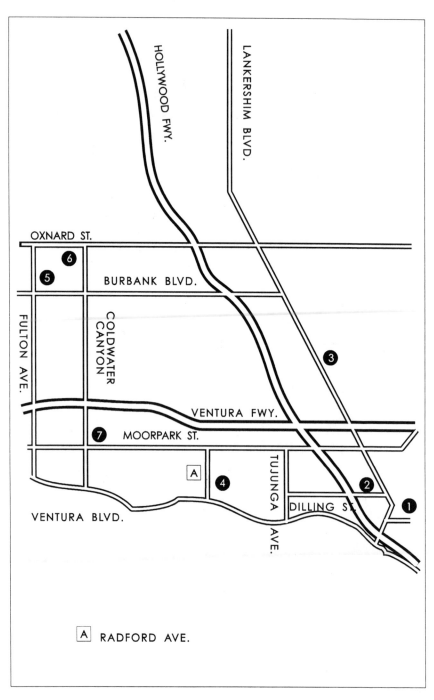

A RADFORD AVE.

MAP 32 **UNIVERSAL CITY, NORTH HOLLYWOOD, & STUDIO CITY**

UNIVERSAL CITY, NORTH HOLLYWOOD AND STUDIO CITY

1. UNIVERSAL STUDIOS HOLLYWOOD, 100 Universal City Plaza, (818) 508-9600

As a tourist attraction, Universal Studios Hollywood ranks second in Southern California only to Disneyland. In fact, it is so popular that the theme park actually makes more money every year for Universal than its movies. Universal offers stunt shows, technical attractions, rides, and a narrated tram tour through Universal's back lot, the largest in the world. The Bates Motel, seen in *Psycho,* is there, as are the sets used in *Back to the Future* (the Hill Valley courthouse), *The Sting,* and quite a few Universal television series, including "Murder She Wrote," "Matlock," "Leave It To Beaver," "The Munsters," and "Nancy Drew." Other highlights include a museum dedicated to Lucille Ball and "Jurassic Park—The Ride," which is particularly popular when temperatures in the San Fernando Valley soar during summertime. Tourists emerge from the ride happily drenched.

Adjacent to the park is Universal CityWalk, a three-block-long entertainment and shopping promenade that has become a popular local and tourist destination in and of itself. CityWalk features entertainment-themed restaurants and shops and a complex of theaters.

2. "THE BRADY BUNCH" HOUSE, 11222 Dilling Street

House used for the exterior of the popular ABC sitcom, which aired from 1969 to 1974. Because a new fence altered the house's appearance, and the new owner refused offers of cash to tear it down, the producers of the movie version did not return here for filming and instead built a facade replicating the house around another house on Firmament Avenue in Sherman Oaks.

3. ACADEMY OF TELEVISION ARTS AND SCIENCES, 5220 Lankershim Boulevard (corner of Magnolia Boulevard)

Only the library is open to the general public, but outside the building itself is a Hall of Fame Plaza featuring bronze statutes of Lucille Ball, Jack Benny, Mary Tyler Moore, and other members of the Academy's Hall of Fame.

4. CBS STUDIO CENTER, 4024 Radford Avenue

This studio has changed hands several times since Mack Sennett, "The King of Comedy," built it in 1928. It has variously been Mascot Pictures, Republic Studios, CBS Television Center, CBS/Fox Studios and CBS/MTM. Many of the most memorable programs in television history have been produced here: "Rawhide," "Gunsmoke," "The Mary Tyler Moore Show," "The Bob Newhart Show," "Rhoda," "Lou Grant," "WKRP in Cincinnati," "Gilligan's Island," "The Wild, Wild West," "My Three Sons," "Hawaii Five-0," "Get Smart," "Hill St. Blues," "St. Elsewhere," "Remington Steele," "Falcon Crest," "Roseanne," "Cybill," "Third Rock From the Sun," and "Seinfeld." No tours; no visitors allowed.

5. LOS ANGELES VALLEY COLLEGE, 5800 Fulton Avenue

Danny DeVito took writing classes from Billy Crystal here in the black comedy *Throw Momma From the Train.*

6. GRANT HIGH SCHOOL, 13000 Oxnard Street (at Coldwater Canyon)

Used for the filming of *Clueless,* which starred Alicia Silverstone, and teen-oriented TV shows, including "The Wonder Years," "Beverly Hills 90210," and "Life Goes On." Alumni include Tom Selleck, Brian Robbins, and Mitch Gaylord.

7. LITTLE BROWN CHURCH IN THE VALLEY, 4418 Coldwater Canyon

Ronald Reagan and Nancy Davis were married here on March 4, 1952.

CELEBRITIES WHO LIVE IN STUDIO CITY: Crystal Bernard, Elayne Boosler, Thomas Calabro, William Daniels and Bonnie Bartlett, Shelley Duvall, Erik Estrada, Helen Hunt, Michael McDonald, Roddy McDowell, Michael J. McKean, Colm Meaney, Alyssa Milano, Jay North, Ted Shakelford, William Shatner, Betty Thomas, and George Wendt.

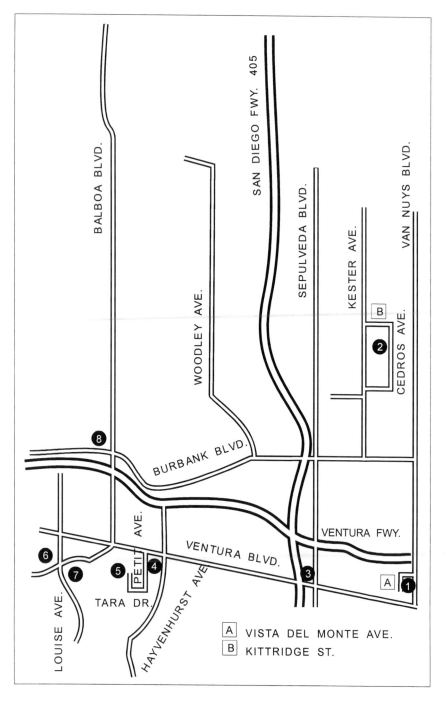

MAP 33 SHERMAN OAKS, VAN NUYS & ENCINO

SHERMAN OAKS, VAN NUYS, AND ENCINO

1. MARILYN MONROE'S FIRST HONEYMOON HOME, 4524 Vista del Monte (one block west of Van Nuys Boulevard)

After marrying her first husband, Jim Dougherty, on June 19, 1942, a 16-year-old Norma Jean Baker (who later changed her name to Marilyn Monroe) lived in a one-room studio apartment here for a few months.

2. VAN NUYS HIGH SCHOOL, 6535 Cedros Avenue

One of the high schools used for the filming of "The Wonder Years" and "Life Goes On." *Fast Times at Ridgemont High* and *My Science Project* were also shot here. Famous alumni include Robert Redford, Don Drysdale, Natalie Wood, Paula Abdul, Stacy Keach, and Jane Russell. Marilyn Monroe attended school here for a year, but was not graduated.

3. SHERMAN OAKS GALLERIA, 15303 Ventura Boulevard

Moon Unit Zappa spoofed this once-notorious teen hangout—and the spoiled, cliquish teen-agers she met at Bar Mitzvah parties—in her hit song "Valley Girls." The Galleria was also the site of the filming of *Fast Times at Ridgemont High, Commando,* and according to one mall official, "a lot of B movies we'd rather not talk about."

4. FORMER HOME OF MICHAEL JACKSON, 4641 Hayvenhurst Avenue

The self-anointed King of Pop moved to the 2,700-acre Neverland Ranch in Santa Barbara in 1988, but this 8,000-square-foot home, where his parents and at least one of his brothers have resided since 1971, is still listed in his name. *Entertainment Weekly* reports that "a metal star engraved with his name is embedded in the walkway to the 20-room mansion, lest anyone forget that this is a house that Michael built and still maintains." In 1993 Los Angeles police officers, investigating allegations that Michael molested young boys, raided the home and seized several boxes of items from his old bedroom.

5. "HOUSE OF TWO GABLES," 4543 Tara Drive

Gable lived here with three of his wives: Carole Lombard, Lady Sylvia Ashley and Kay Williams Spreckles. In 1977 the home was purchased by Michael R. Milken.

6. HOME OF KIRSTIE ALLEY, 4875 Louise Avenue

Alley lives in a mansion that Barbara Walters called "one of the loveliest homes I've ever seen." We do not know if she kept her promise, but according to Walters, Kirstie vowed to spend $400 a week on flowers in the home—the amount she used to spend for cocaine.

Al Jolson originally built the house for Ruby Keeler. Alley also owns a 300-acre ranch in Oregon and a 20-bedroom ocean-front home in Maine.

7. LONG-TIME HOME OF JOHN WAYNE, 4750 Louise Avenue

Wayne, a chain-smoker, lived here until he was stricken with lung cancer and decided to move to Newport

Beach, where the air is easier to breathe. He lived here with his second wife, former call girl Esperanza "Chata" Bauer, and his third wife, Pilar Palette, from 1951 to 1965.

8. BALBOA PARK, Balboa and Burbank Boulevards
The park is not exactly what you would call a tourist attraction—unless, of course, you go on Saturdays to root for Michael Keaton, Tony Danza, Billy Crystal, and the other show business celebrities playing in the ShowBiz Softball League. Games are held on four diamonds every two hours between 9:00 A.M. and 5:00 P.M. NBC, Warner Bros., 20th Century Fox and other studios sponsor teams.

JUST OFF THE MAP, in the northwest part of the San Fernando Valley, are a few sites that are historic for reasons other than entertainment. The 6.7-on-the-Richter-scale January 17, 1994 earthquake which devastated Los Angeles had its epicenter in the community of Northridge. 16 of the 57 deaths occurred when the top floors of the Northridge Meadows Apartments at 9565 Reseda Boulevard collapsed on the bottom floor, killing tenants sleeping on the first level. The building has since been razed.

Also off the map is the site of the March 3, 1991, Rodney King beating incident, which occurred on a dirt field across from the Mountainback Apartments at 11777 Foothill Boulevard in Lakeview Terrace. It was the most publicized incident of police brutality in the nation. The April 28, 1992, acquittal of the four police officers who clubbed King 56 times led to the worst riots ever in the United States. (Two of the officers, Stacy Koon and Lawrence Powell, were subsequently convicted of federal charges.)

There are a few other movie and TV locations in the northern San Fernando Valley. The Ewing house featured on the "Dynasty" spin-off "Knots Landing" can be found on Crystalaire Place in Granada Hills. And at 11600 Eldridge Avenue in Lakeview Terrace, not far from the King beating site, is the former Lakeview Medical Center. The building would have been the Nancy Reagan Drug Center, but the residents of Lakeview Terrace, who objected to placing the center in their neighborhood, threatened to picket the Reagan Bel-Air mansion. Nancy withdrew her support for the project, and the building is now used exclusively for motion picture and television filming. Lakeview served as Pescadero State Hospital in *Terminator II*—the hospital where a crazed Linda Hamilton was imprisoned and the two Terminators had one of their many violent confrontations. The hospital was also seen as both hospitals in *Postcards from the Edge*, and was used for scenes in *Mr. Jones, Ricochet, Dying Young, Another 48 Hours, Heart Condition, She's Having a Baby,* and *Road House.*

In the western end of the Valley, Taft High School at 5461 Winnetka Ave. in Woodland Hills was transformed into West Dale High School for *The Brady Bunch Movie.* Taft alumni include Kathleen Sullivan and Lisa Kudrow.

CELEBRITIES WHO LIVE IN THE SAN FERNANDO VALLEY: Sherman Oaks residents include Albert Brooks, Gabrielle Carteris, Michael Chiklis, Robert Conrad, Ronnie Cox, Michael Dorn, Hector Elizondo, Gregory Harrison, James Earl Jones, Steve Kanaly, DeForest Kelly, David Leisure, Gavin MacLeod, and Kristy McNichol.

Steve Allen, Ernie Banks, LeVar Burton, Dana Carvey, Richard Crenna, Tony Danza, William Devane, Patti Duke, Annette Funicello, Sara Gilbert, Robert Guillame, David Hasselhoff, Samuel L. Jackson, Al Jarreau, Melissa Manchester, Graham Nash, Edward James Olmos, Tom Petty, Tim and Daphne Reid, Smokey Robinson, Pat Sajak, Cybill Shepherd, Jean Smart, Patrick Swayze, and Leslie Anne Warren live in Encino.

James Doohan and Walter Koenig live in Van Nuys. Alec Baldwin, Kim Basinger, Elgin Baylor, James Brown, Greg Evigan, Nichele Nichols, and Suzanne Somers own homes in Woodland Hills. Tony Danza, Patrick Duffy, Martin Kove, and Nicholas Turturro live in Tarzana. Tom Arnold, Kelsey Grammer, and Charlie Sheen live in Agoura Hills.

Other Valley residents include Lisa Bonet, Bruce Boxleitner, Beau Bridges, Natalie Cole, John Davidson, Bob Eubanks, Ted Lange, Matt LeBlanc, Clayton Moore, Mickey Rooney, Jack Scalia, Donna Summer, and JoBeth Williams.

When Steven Spielberg's locations scouts searched for a house to use as Elliott's in *E.T.*, they looked for a typical suburban house that looked like it had a magical mountain and a redwood forest behind it. They found the house in the northwest section of the San Fernando Valley (7121 Lonzo Street, Tujunga), situated in front of one of the highest peaks of the San Gabriel Mountains. E.T. took up residence here after being stranded by his fellow travelers, and Elliott hid him until both were discovered by government agents. The Halloween street scenes and the chase scenes, though, were filmed on several different streets of Porter Ranch, another community in the northwestern portion of the San Fernando Valley. The famous scene in which Elliott and his friends, seemingly cornered by police cars, fly away into the air on their bicycles was filmed on White Oak Drive in Northridge, between Tribune and San Fernando Mission Roads.

238

OTHER POINTS OF INTEREST IN OR NEAR LOS ANGELES

- **MALIBU CREEK STATE PARK,** Las Virgenes Road, Malibu

  This park was once Century Ranch, a Twentieth Century Fox back lot. It was purchased by the State of California in 1974 and continues to be a frequent filming site. The park was where incoming choppers brought in the wounded in television's "M*A*S*H" (as well as in the 1970 movie of the same name). The park has also been the site of the first and at least one *Planet of the Apes* sequel, *Butch Cassidy and the Sundance Kid,* and *Tora! Tora! Tora!*

- **PARAMOUNT RANCH**, 1813 Cornell Road, Agoura (north of Malibu Creek State Park)

  This national park was once owned by Paramount Studios. Still in existence is a "Western Town," which includes a general store, wood shop, barn and bridge used in the filming of "The Virginian," "Have Gun, Will Travel," "The Riflemen," "Bat Masterson," "Dr. Quinn, Medicine Woman," and dozens of other films and television series. Free tours are given on an irregular basis. Call (818) 597-9192 for additional information.

- **SIX FLAGS MAGIC MOUNTAIN,** 26101 Magic Mountain Parkway, off Interstate 5, (805) 255-4111

  The amusement park was turned into Wally World in *National Lampoon's Vacation.* It has also doubled as Wisconsin Wonderland, the amusement park seen in the opening credits of the ABC sitcom "Step by Step," which starred Patrick Duffy and Suzanne Somers.

- **VASQUEZ ROCKS COUNTY PARK,** 10700 Escondido Canyon Road, Agua Dulce (northeast of Newhall on Route 14)

  Fodors calls it "one of Los Angeles County's best photo opportunities [even though it's almost] a two-hour drive from downtown." The main attraction are the unusual angular rocks that one might expect to encounter on an alien planet. Dozens of Western and science fiction movies (including *Star Trek IV, Star Wars* and *Starship Troopers*), and television shows (the original "Star Trek") have been filmed there. The city of Bedrock in *The Flintstones* was also built by the rocks.

- **"NIGHTMARE ON ELM STREET" HOUSE,** 1428 N. Genesee Avenue, Hollywood

  The two-story white house where Freddy Krueger ran amok is located in Hollywood, just south of Nichols Canyon.

- **HOUSE AT 1530 ORANGE GROVE AVENUE,** Hollywood

  Jamie Lee Curtis lived here in *Halloween.* The street, two blocks west of Genesee, is used frequently as a filming site because it does not have palm trees and looks midwestern.

- **"MUSIC BOX" STAIRS,** 900 block of Vendome Street, Silver Lake

  In the Academy Award-winning 1932 film short *The Music Box*, Laurel and Hardy, playing bumbling piano delivery men, tried to move a piano up these stairs. The steps are located just south of Sunset Boulevard between Descanso Drive and Vendome Street.

- **USC/COUNTY HOSPITAL,** 1200 N. State Street, East Los Angeles

  Port Charles Hospital in "General Hospital."

- **SHOOTING OF MARVIN GAYE,** 2101 S. Gramercy Place

  On April 1, 1984, the singer was shot to death by his father, Reverend Marvin Gaye, Sr., in Mid-City, a community south of Hancock Park.

- **HUNTINGTON PARK HIGH SCHOOL,** 6020 Miles Avenue, Huntington Park

  Most of the scenes from the musical *Grease,* starring John Travolta and Olivia Newton-John, filmed here, including the dance, the principal's office, the auto shop and the bleachers (although not the final carnival scene). The school is located six miles southeast of downtown Los Angeles.

- **GARFIELD HIGH SCHOOL,** 5101 E. Sixth Street

  The movie *Stand and Deliver* was based on a true story about this East Los Angeles school. The students, underprivileged and expected to underperform, were taught to excel in calculus for a state test by a teacher, Jaime Escalante, who was portrayed in the movie by Edward James Olmos. When the students performed well above average, the state testing agency accused the students of cheating and invalidated the scores. Given the choice of either accepting the testing service's decision or retesting, the students chose to "stand and deliver."

- **PUENTE HILLS MALL**, Colima Road, Puente Hills
  In the original *Back to the Future*, Christopher Lloyd was gunned down by terrorists, and Michael J. Fox took Lloyd's DeLorean back in time, in the parking lot of the J. C. Penney's at the mall. The high school featured in the movie was Whittier High School, 12417 Philadelphia Street, Whittier.

- **MONROVIA CITY HALL**, 415 S. Ivy, Monrovia
  Was transformed into the Rome, Wisconsin courthouse in the acclaimed CBS drama "Picket Fences." The police station was located next door at 140 East Lime. Tom Skerritt and Kathy Baker's house was at 211 North Highland.

- **SHAMROCK MEATS**, 3461 E. Vernon Avenue (corner Alcoa Avenue), Vernon
  In the first *Rocky*, Sylvester Stallone worked here and practiced for prize fights by punching slabs of beef. Scenes from *The Mambo Kings* were also shot here.

- **KERN'S OF CALIFORNIA**, 13010 East Temple Avenue, City of Industry
  In the first *Terminator*, Arnold Schwarzenegger was crushed to death in this food manufacturing and canning facility.

- **VENICE HIGH SCHOOL,** 13000 Venice Boulevard, Venice

  Was also used as Rydell High School in *Grease*. There is a statue of Myrna Loy, a Warner Bros. star of the 1920s and a former Venice High School student, on the front lawn.

- **LOS ANGELES INTERNATIONAL AIRPORT**

  Airplane! is probably the most famous of the many movies filmed at LAX.

- **PORTOFINO INN,** 260 Portofino Way, Redondo Beach

  In *Cannonball Run*, starring Burt Reynolds and dozens of other stars, the finish line of the cross-country speed car race was filmed extensively here. The hotel was also "Hotel Malibu" in the short-lived TV series of that name.

- **KING HARBOR**, Beryl Street, Redondo Beach

  Setting of the NBC crime show "Riptide," which aired between 1984 and 1986.

- **HAWTHORNE GRILL**, 13763 S. Hawthorne Boulevard, Hawthorne

  In *Pulp Fiction*, Amanda Plummer and Tim Roth robbed this restaurant, only to run into hit men John Travolta and Samuel L. Jackson.

- **TORRANCE HIGH SCHOOL,** 2200 West Carson Street, Torrance

  The high school depicted as West Beverly High in the early years of "Beverly Hills 90210."

- **WAYFARER'S CHAPEL,** 5755 Palos Verdes Drive South, Rancho Palos Verdes

    This unique glass-walled chapel, designed by Lloyd Wright, Frank Lloyd Wright's son, is a popular tourist attraction and is used frequently for movie wedding scenes, including Dennis Quaid and Meg Ryan's wedding in *Innerspace*. In real life "Beach Boy" Brian Wilson, Jayne Mansfield, Dennis Hopper, and "M*A*S*H" star Gary Burghoff were married here.

- **QUEEN MARY,** Pier J at the end of Long Beach Freeway, Long Beach

    The Queen Mary, one of the largest passenger liners ever built, has been in over 200 productions, most notably *The Poseidon Adventure*. In *Someone to Watch Over Me*, Mimi Rogers witnessed a murder in the swimming pool, which was transformed into a New York art museum (the producers put plexiglass over the pool).

    The huge white geodesic dome next door, which once housed Howard Hughes' famous seaplane, the Spruce Goose, has sometimes been rented to movie companies. The space station in *Stargate* and the Bat Cave and the Riddler's Lair in *Batman Forever* were built there.

- **HYATT REGENCY HOTEL**, 200 S. Pine Avenue, Long Beach

    The most entertaining and preposterous action sequences in *Last Action Hero* were staged on the hotel's roof, where Arnold Schwarzenegger crashed a gangster's funeral, stole the corpse, and while dodging the mourners' gunfire, jumped onto an outdoor glass elevator (added especially for the movie), only to have to dodge artillery fire from a helicopter. Schwarzenegger shot out the helicopter, but the elevator collapsed, forcing him to make a midair grab onto the corpse, which dangled from a conveniently placed crane. Schwarzengger fell again, this time into a specially created Hollywood version of the La Brea Tar Pits (actually a mulch made with Oreo cookie dye). Fortunately, Schwarzenegger's movie daughter arrived just in time with a change of clothes.

- **VETERANS ADMINISTRATION MEDICAL CENTER,** 5901 E. Seventh Street (at Pacific Coast Highway), Long Beach
  The VA Hospital's facade is depicted as "Wilshire Memorial Hospital" in "Melrose Place."

- **SANTA ANA TRAIN STATION,** 1000 E. Santa Ana Boulevard, Santa Ana
  The place where Tom Cruise said goodbye to Dustin Hoffman in the final scene of *Rainman;* and where Chevy Chase, accompanied by Darryl Hannah, eluded his pursuers in *Memoirs of an Invisible Man.*

- **MAIN PLACE, SANTA ANA,** 2800 N. Main Street, Santa Ana
  The mall where Arnold Schwarzenegger arrested Richard Tyson in *Kindergarten Cop.*

- **HOAG HOSPITAL,** 301 Newport Avenue, Newport Beach
  The exterior was depicted as the Miami hospital in the NBC comedy "Empty Nest" and its spin-off "Nurses."

- **MEDIEVAL TIMES RESTAURANT,** 7662 Beach Boulevard, Buena Park
  In *The Cable Guy*, Matthew Broderick defended

himself from the volent assualts of his new friend, Jim Carrey.

- **TODAY'S MEMORIES**, 129 N. Glassell Street, Orange

This antique store, which appeared as Patterson's Appliances, was the principal location in Tom Hanks' directorial debut, *That Thing You Do!* Over 40 stores on Glassell Street and Chapman Avenue in downtown Orange were dressed up to appear as Erie, Pennsylvania in 1964.

ACKNOWLEDGMENTS

There are so many people that I need to thank that it is difficult to know where to start. In researching this book, I interviewed or consulted with many location managers, operators of location services, publicists, librarians, realtors, and other entertainment industry professionals.

Perhaps it would be fitting to start with the members of the various city and state film commissions: Dirk Beving and his staff at the City of Los Angeles Film and Video Permit Office; Lisa Mosher, librarian; Hugh Cooper, permit coordinator, and Amy Gutierrez, intern at the California Film Commission; Jason Hartman of the Los Angeles County Film Office; Ariel Penn, film liaison, city of Pasadena; Benita Miller, special event coordinator of Beverly Hills' Department of Public Services; Ian Tanza of the West Hollywood Film Commission; Christopher Reed, the former permit coordinator of Culver City; Richard Wiles, the battallion chief who issues permits for the city of Vernon; and Cheryl Adams of the Santa Clarita Film Commission.

I would like to especially thank Diane Klein, Antoinette Levine, Robin Citrin, Donald Potts, Jack English, Joseph Luizzi, Sr., and the other location managers, location scouts and operators of location services who helped me: Ned Shapiro, Steve Dawson, David Israel, Louis Goldstein, Paul Pav, Richard Davis, Bud Aronson, Annette Gahret, Peter Juliano, Billie

Jenkins, Marie Warren, Bruce Rush, Keith Kramer, Craig Pointes, Richard Rosenberg, Marvin Bernstein, Bob Craft, Amy Ness, Rhonda Baer, Taman McCall, David Preston, Ken Campbell, Mike Alvarado, Ken Rosen, Rick Rosen, Steph Benseman, Rowland Kirks, Ed Jeffers, Eva Schroeder, and Kris Wagner.

As well, Randy Young, past president of the Pacific Palisades Historical Society; Phyllis Lerner of the Beverly Hills Historical Society; Hope Keimon and Tonie Carnes of the Pasadena Historical Society; Betsy Goldman of the Venice Historical Society; Linda Brady of the Culver City Historical Society; Julie Lugocerra, Sony Pictures' liaison with the community and author of a forthcoming book on Culver City; Louise Gabriel of the Santa Monica Historical Society; and Dorothy Price and Sid Adair of the Windsor Square-Hancock Park Historical Society, were all very generous with their time and provided very helpful information.

Thanks also to the librarians who helped me research various topics, including Lisa Mosher of the California Film Commission; the staff of the Center for Motion Picture Studies in Beverly Hills; Shirley Kennedy and her staff at the Academy of Television Arts and Sciences; the librarians at the Los Angeles Public Library, Pasadena Public Library, and the Orange County Public Library, particularly the El Toro branch; Raymond Soto, UCLA Film and Television Librarian; Jennie Watts and Julie Yamamoto of the Huntington Library; Ken Kenyon of 20th Century Fox; Alline Merchant of the Brand Library; Tim Gregory of the Pasadena Historical Society; and Robert Tieman, assistant archivist, Walt Disney Studios.

Gary Sherwin, former director of media relations, and Connie Eldridge of the Los Angeles Convention and

Visitors Bureau, were most helpful; as were Jill Singer of the Donahue Group, which represents the Beverly Hills Visitors Bureau, and Victoria King of the Hotel Bel-Air. A number of other public relations professionals gave generously of their time, including Andy Marx; Lindsey Jones; Saul Kahan; Michael Klastorin; Paul Gendreau; Chris Tomasko; Denise Greenawalt; Doug Taylor; Liz Gengl; Richard Neely; John West; Fred Howard; Jill Tsukatoma; Rich Bornstein; Georgianna Francisco; Tom Gray; Teri Bond Michael, Karen Mack, Mary Tokita and James Blaine of UCLA; Tom Witherspoon of the Queen Mary; Diane Barnhart of Caltech; Mary Blaze of Beverly Hills Hotel; Karen Wong of the Santa Monica Convention and Visitors Bureau; Harry Medved of the Screen Actors Guild; Kelly Greene of the Hollywood Roosevelt Hotel; Cliff Gallo of the American Film Institute; Kenlyn Elipsen of the Huntington; LuAnn Munns of Los Angeles State and County Arboretum; Barbara Leigh of the former St. James Club; Maureen Stokes of The Biltmore (and David Morgan, who oversees filming there); Jim Yeager, director of publicity, Universal Studios Hollywood; Mike Rosenberg of the Los Angeles Coliseum; Julie Taylor of the Pacific Design Center; Rick Stevens of the California Highway Patrol; and Jeff Bliss of Pepperdine.

And I certainly have not forgotten Marsha Meyer Sculatti of the West Hollywood Marketing Associaton; Luc Tamarra of the Los Angeles Unified School District; Kari Johnson, curator of the Hollywood Studio Museum; Al Davis, general manager of the Magic Castle; Mrs. Jay (Ramona) Ward of Dudley Doo-Rite Emporium; Nicky Blair; Denise Carrejo of Damar; Dee Stanley, Walker Location Services; Kevin Beggs of the "Baywatch" production staff; Doug MacArthur, former manager of the Yamashiro; Judy Hunter, executive director of the

Pasadena Historical Society; Don Zepfel, vice president, production, Universal Studios; Mary Fry, general manager and Beth Savage, executive assistant of Raleigh Studios; Lorraine Shaw, business affairs, and Richard Schnyder, vice president, sales, Hollywood Center Studios, business affairs; Debbie Ross, manager of the Montecito Apartments; Ana Martinez-Holler of the Hollywood Walk of Fame; Manny Weltman, whose passion for historical accuracy should be shared by more chroniclers of Hollywood history; Stephanie Pond-Smith of Carolco; Eileen Garcia, president of the South Pasadena Chamber of Commerce; Steve Rose, president of the Culver City Chamber of Commerce; Dee Powers, owner of the Port Cafe; Josh Avin and Jason Vance of the Hotel Mondrian; Randall Makinson, director and curator of the Gamble House; Timothy Buchanan, principal of Burroughs High School; Don Waldrop, president, Franklin Hills Residents Association; Raoul H. Pinno, film and photo shoot manager, UCLA; Patricia Cohen Samuels of Spago; Richard Terra, vice president, Shamrock Meats; Nelson Crispo, USC film coordinator; Steve Harris, manager of the Castle Green Apartments, Pasadena; Norma Tomkinson of the J. W. Marriott Hotel; Tom O'Brien, personnel director, Kern's of California; Jane Gilman, editor of the *Larchmont Chronicle*; Rick Rossini, assistant principal, Van Nuys High School; Tom Buckley, film coordinator of Union Station; Abel Ramirez, manager of Caltech's Atheneum; Susan Thompson of the Westin Bonaventure; Ruth Richards of the South Pasadena Preservation Society; Andy Stamatin of the Shrine Auditorium; Robin Faulk, marketing director, Santa Monica Place; Joe Walker, assistant principal, Grant High School; Bob Sirchia, vice president of Culver Studios; Ellen West and Ed Giles of the Department of Water and

Power; Mark Stokhaug, director of security for 444 S. Flower Street; Richard Adkins, executive director, Hollywood Studio Museum; Ruth Ryon and Steve Harvey of the Los Angeles Times; Richard Taylor, head of fire and security, Warner Hollywood Studios; Tracy Fowler of the Century Plaza Hotel and Towers; Barbara Rosenman of Los Angeles Parks and Recreation (Greystone); Joseph DiSante, manager of guest services, ABC-TV; Stephanie DeWolf, assistant planner, and Randy Shulman, planning intern, of the Pasadena Urban Conservation Department; Officer Chuck Foote, Los Angeles Police Academy; Sgt. Larry Thompson, Los Angeles Police Department film coordinator; Richard Munitz, assistant principal, Beverly Hills High School; Marge Maple and Nancy O'Connor of Hollywood Memorial Park Cemetery; Karen Sanders of the Pasadena Convention and Visitors Bureau; Norma LeValley, editor, *South Pasadena Review;* Charlie Morton, former owner of the "Dynasty" house; Peter Pampush, assistant director, student affairs, USC School of Cinema and Television; Bob Bacon of Ramsey-Shilling Realtors; Deborah Bieber and Denise Mathis of Bellefontaine School; Sandra Griffin, property manager of the El Royale Apartments; David Bowen of "Step by Step," Jodi Hutchinson of Six Flags Magic Mountain; Judy Bijlani, marketing director, Main Place, Santa Ana; Cecyle Rexrode, Shirley Krims and David Horowitz of Warner Bros.; Connie Humburger of LA Conservancy; Carolyn Lucci of the Sherman Oaks Galleria; Paul Garcia, buildings and grounds manager of the Wayfarers Chapel; Ellen Appel Public Relations; Larry Paull; Emily Ferry; Marcia Reed and Jim Bissel.

For helping me keep the book up to date, I would like to thank Laurie Jacobson, the author of *Hollywood Haunted* and *Hollywood Heartbreak;* realtor Elaine

251

Young; Adam Gooch of Southland Title; Rachel Smookler and Monica Poling of the Hollywood Entertainment Museum; Marcia Tyselling of Star Wares; Erik Porter of the Malibu Film Office; Steve Lawler, project manager of filming at the Ambassador Hotel; Geri Pitt of the Four Seasons at Beverly Hills; Karen Millet of Victoria King Public Relations; Lisa Baur of the Park Plaza Hotel; Pamela Bellew of Occidental College; Frank Cooper of the Art Deco Society; Kirk Slaughter of Castle Ivar; Tony Garcia, principal, Huntington Park High School; Ben Jacobs, principal, Venice High School; and Steve Millar, John P. Crumlish, Ralph Chaump, and Mick Lehr, who provided film and TV locations. Scott Carter took me on a memorable tour of movie sites of South Pasadena.

Jeff Huttner, author of *The LA Bargain Book*, and his assistant Linda Roberts; Kathryn Leigh Scott of Pomegranate Press; Julie von Zerneck and Joseph Naud of Portrait of a Bookstore; Stephanie Jones of the Automobile Club of Southern California; Karen Perea of Barnes & Noble; Steven Abrams; Paul Keane; Ronnie Silverstone; and Margaret Fishman all provided valuable advice which I appreciate.

And finally, I'd like to thank those involved in the production of this book, including my editor, Lisa Rojany, for her invaluable and painstaking editorial expertise; Ron Fishman and Adam Fishman, for their invaluable computer assistance; and Julian Wasser, who provided many of the photographs included here.

My apologies to anyone I inadvertently left out.

A NOTE ABOUT FUTURE EDITIONS

The Ultimate Hollywood Tour Book is updated annually, and future editions will include the latest filming locations, as well as updated listings and additional points of interest.

If you know of a filming location or other site not mentioned in this book—and if we use the information, subject, of course, to verification—we will send you a free copy of the next edition of the book.

Tips should be sent to:

North Ridge Books
P. O. Box 1463
El Toro, CA 92630

ABOUT THE AUTHOR

William A. Gordon is a writer, publisher, and author of three previous books, including *Shot on This Site,* a guide to more than 900 film and TV locations throughout the United States.

His acclaimed study of the May 4, 1970, killings at Kent State University and the subsequent trials, *Four Dead in Ohio: Was There a Conspiracy at Kent Study?*, was praised by *Choice m*agazine "as entertaining as the best detective fiction and as analytical and well documented as the best journalism or scholarship."

Wilson Library Bulletin called his book, *"How Many Books Do You Sell in Ohio?": A Quote Book for Writers* "irresistible," and said "Gordon has succeeded in selecting the most memorable, thought-provoking, important, funny and/or outrageous quotations about the book world." (The title, incidentally, is one of the quotations in the book.)

Mr. Gordon frequently lectures about the best ways to sightsee in Los Angeles and has made numerous media appearances. He currently lives in a suburb of Los Angeles.

INDEX

ABC Entertainment Center, 110
ABC Television Center, 195
A & M Records, 146
Abdul, Paula, 66, 179, 233
Academy of Television Arts and Sciences, 230
Adams, Madame Alex, 47, 130
Adkins, Richard, 156
"Adventures of Ozzie and Harriet," 163
African Queen, The, 219
Against All Odds, 107
Airplane!, 243
All Saints Church, 61
Allen, Woody, 122, 137
Alley, Kirstie, 234
Ambassador Hotel, 173
American Film Institute, 20, 192
Amsterdam, Morey, 19
Andersen, Christopher, 87
Anderson, Loni, 39, 179
Andrews, Julie, 56, 72, 86
Annie Hall, 122
Alto-Nido Apartments, 155
Arachnophobia, 212
Argyle Hotel, 123, 124
Astaire, Fred, 29

Babylon, 196

Back to the Future series, 9, 143, 211, 217, 213, 229, 242
Balboa Park, 235
Ball, Lucile, 30, 38, 136, 221, 229, 230
Baldwin, Alec, 136
Ballerina Clown, 96
Banks, Jonathan, 214
Barney's Beanery, 134
Barrymore, John, 29
Basinger, Kim, 136
Basten, Fred, 120
"Batman" (television series), 191, 210
Batman (feature film), 191
Batman Forever, 244
"Battle of the Network Stars," 85
"Baywatch," 102
Beatles, The, 40, 49, 130, 156, 201
Beatty, Warren, 58, 65, 122, 136, 148, 179
Beck, Marilyn, 46
Beethoven, 217
Begelman, David, 58, 173
Belushi, John, 10, 121, 122, 129
Bening, Annette, 58, 136, 179
Benny, Jack, 37, 55, 106, 230
"Benson," 213
Bergen, Candice, 10, 26, 30, 32, 41

Being There, 211
Berle, Milton, 24, 155
Beverly Center, 137
"Beverly Hillbillies, The" (television series), 42-3, 44, 163
Beverly Hillbillies, The (movie), 113, 213
Beverly Hills Cop, 9, 46, 203, 212, 214
Beverly Hills Cop II, 57, 151, 152, 200, 212, 214
Beverly Hills High School, 113
Beverly Hills Hotel, 19, 21-2, 23, 120
"Beverly Hills 90210," 53, 101, 113, 218, 231, 242
Beverly Hills Visitors Bureau, 64
Beverly Hilton Hotel, 100, 114
Beverly Park, 179, 181
Big Fix, The, 109
Biltmore Hotel, Regal, 171, 201-2
Black Rain, 195, 200
Blade Runner, 195, 202, 205
Black Sunday, 208
Blanc, Mel, 107, 160, 161
Blocker, Dan, 172
Blue Chips, 208
Blue Jay Way, 130
Blumenthal, John, 152
Bochco, Steven, 76
Body Double, 183
Bogart, Humphrey, 36, 54, 61, 119, 128, 135
"Bonanza," 71, 142, 191
Boone, Pat, 24
Borofsky, Jonathan, 96

Bow, Clara, 61, 119
Boyer, Peter J., 221-2
Bradbury Building, 200
"Brady Bunch, The," 10, 230
Brady Bunch Movie, The, 236
Branaugh, Kenneth, 210
Brando, Christian, 181
Brando, Marlon, 29, 43, 145, 181
Brenneman, Amy, 100
Broad Beach, 89-90, 92
Bronson Caves, 191
Brooks, Mel, 83, 103, 201, 218
Brosnan, Pierce, 91, 111, 136
Brown Simpson, Nicole, 63, 67, 69, 71, 98, 199
Bruckheimer, Jerry, 46, 82
Bryson Apartment Hotel, 174
Buffy the Vampire Slayer, 175, 195
Bugsy, 58, 60, 175, 201, 205, 213
Burke, Delta, 202
Burns, George 63
Burroughs, Edgar Rice, 48
Burroughs High School, John, 223
Burton, Tim, 152, 154
Bush, George, 86

Cable Guy, The, 245
Cage, Nicolas, 113, 172, 191
"Cagney and Lacey," 198, 203
California Institute of Technology (Caltech), 214
Cannonball Run, 243
Capitol Records, 156, 157
Capote, Truman, 49, 110
Carbon Beach, 82, 83

Carnes, Toni, 210
Carolco Pictures, 62
Carrey, Jim, 146, 246
Carson, Joanna, 42
Carson, Joanne, 49
Carson, Johnny, 42, 49, 82, 87, 88, 223
Castillo del Lago, 188
Castle Green Apartments, 213
CBS, 158167
CBS/MTM Studios, 230
Cedars-Sinai Medical Center, 136
Center for Motion Picture Studies, 66
Century City Shopping Center, 110, 112
Century Plaza Hotel, 110
Century Plaza Towers, 111, 112
Chandler Pavilion, Dorothy, 198
Chaplin, Charlie, 25, 146, 159
Chateau Marmont, 118, 120, 121
"Cheers," 147
Chemosphere, 183, 185
Cher, 36, 41-2, 55, 89
Chinatown, 189, 202
"CHIPs," 207
Cinerama Dome, 156
Ciros, 125
City Hall, Beverly Hills, 62
City Hall, Los Angeles, 203, 204
City Hall, Monrovia, 244
City Hall, Pasadena, 212
Clark, Dick, 86
Clark Productions, Dick, 223
Clayburgh, Jill, 122
Clooney, George, 37

Clooney, Rosemary, 38
Clueless, 231
"The Colbys," 40
Cohn, Harry, 160
Cole, Nat King, 172
Columbia Pictures, 25, 58, 105, 160, 172
Comedy Store, 125
Coming to America, 215
Commando, 234
Crane, Cheryl, 60
Crawford, Joan, 61, 69
Creative Artists Agency (CAA), 114
Criminals Court Building, 199
Crosby, Bing, 53, 106, 226
Cruise, Tom, 200, 245
Crystal, Billy, 137, 144, 231, 244
Culbertson, Judi, 221
Culver Studios, 105
Curtis, Jamie Lee, 113, 135, 239
Curtis, Tony, 55
"Cybill," 230

Daniels, Jeff, 202, 212
Davies, Marion, 101
Davis, Bette, 134, 189, 221
Davis, Marvin, 22
Davis, Jr., Sammy, 24, 25, 29, 57, 134, 221
Day, Doris, 31, 67, 189
Dead Again, 143, 144, 210
Dead Man's Curve, 107
Dean, James, 109, 192
Dean, John, 10, 27
Death Wish, 215
Defending Your Life, 174
DeMille, Cecil B., 105, 142, 146, 159

DeNiro, Robert, 100, 200
"Dennis the Menace," 213
DePalma, Brian, 183
Department of Power and
Water, 198
Depp, Johnny, 122, 123, 128
200
DeVito, Danny, 89,195, 231
Die Hard, 111, 112
Die Hard II, 203
DiMaggio, Joe, 66, 129
Dino's Lodge, 126
Disney Studios, 151, 196,
221-2, 230
Disney, Walt, 40, 196
Doc Hollywood, 126
Doctor, The, 83
"Dr. Quinn, Medicine
Woman," 239
Doheny Estate, 20
Donahue, Phil, 19
D'Onofrio, Vincent, 217
Doors, The, 107, 122, 125,
207
Dougherty, Jim, 237
Douglas, Michael, 103
Down and Out in Beverly
Hills, 60
Downey, Robert, Jr., 90
"Dragnet," 203, 205, 222
Dreyfuss, Richard, 60, 111,
183
Drollet, Dag, 181
"Dynasty," 10, 21, 53, 134,
216, 236
Duck Soup, 215
Duke, Doris, 33
Dunne, Dominique, 109
Duvall, Robert, 103

E! Entertainment, 169

Earhart, Amelia, 226
Earthquake, 189
Ed Wood, 154
Edwards and Hunt, 215
Edwards, Anthony, 77, 109,
168
Edwards, Blake, 56, 86, 184
Edwards, Anne, 129
Edwards, Ralph, 89
Egyptian Theater, 153, 203
El Capitan Theater, 151
El Royale Apartments, 171
"Eleanor and Franklin," 211
"Empty Nest," 245
Emser Rugs and Tile, 134
Ennis-Brown House, 193, 195
Escalante, Jaime, 240
E.T., 106, 238
Exner, Judith Campbell, 118,
133
Eyeman, Scott, 28

Fabulous Baker Boys, The, 20,
58, 151, 201
Factor exhbit, Max, 147
Factor Museum, Max, 151
Fairbanks, Douglas Jr., 75
Fairbanks, Douglas Sr., 24,
28, 101, 159
Falcon Lair, 33
Falk, Peter, 37
Falling Down, 103
"Family," 217
"Fantasy Island," 53, 219
Farmers Market, 167
Farrow, Mia, 39
Fast Times at Ridgemont
High, 233
Father of the Bride, 41, 214
Fein, Art, 86, 107, 125, 130
Fenyes Mansion, 211

Ferrer, Jose, 37
Final Analysis, 109, 200
First Interstate Building, 200-1
First United Methodist
Church, 143
Fisher, Carrie, 56, 113
Fitzgerald, F. Scott, 119
Fleiss, Heidi, 30, 47, 195
Flynn, Errol, 119, 123, 183
Flynt, Larry, 42
Fonda, Bridget, 41
Fonda, Henry, 49
Fonda, Jane, 48, 102
Ford, Harrison, 146, 195, 202
Forest Lawn Memorial Park,
221
Formosa Cafe, 135
Forrest Gump, 64, 174, 208
Forsythe, John, 76
Foul Play, 207, 212
Fox, Michael J., 126, 136,
217, 242
Fox Plaza, 111, 112
Fox Television Center, 159
Fox, Vivica A., 199
Frederick's of Hollywood,
154-5
Frewin, Leslie, 135
Fun With Dick and Jane, 128

Gable, Clark, 49, 64, 119, 123,
134, 135, 172, 234
Gabor, Zsa Zsa, 43, 66, 123
Gaines, Steve, 98
Gamble House, 211, 212, 217
Garcia, Andy, 99
Garden of Allah, 119, 129
Garland, Beverly, 226
Garland, Judy, 49, 56, 129,
152, 155
Garson, Greer, 46

Gaye, Marvin, 241
Gaynor, Janet, 151
Geffen, David, 30, 33, 36, 82
"General Hospital," 215, 241
Gere, Richard, 65, 99, 154
Gershwin, George, 37
Gershwin, Ira, 37
Getty Museum, J. Paul, 78
Getty, J. Paul, 173
Ghost Dad, 217
Ghostbusters, 20, 201
Ghostbusters II, 201
Giancana, Sam, 133
Gibson, Mel, 83, 89, 111, 134,
146, 183, 184
Glover, Crispin, 113, 217
Glover, Danny, 111, 225
Goldberg, Whoopi, 76, 146
Goldman, Ron, 67, 69, 71, 98,
199
Gotcha!, 109, 200
Gould, Elliott, 143
Gower Gulch, 158
Grand Canyon, 193, 205
Grant, Cary, 46, 75, 102
Grant High School, 231
Grauman, Sid, 146, 154, 204
Grease, 195, 241, 243
Green Acres, 30-1
Greene, Lorne, 71
Greer, Robin, 63
Greystone Mansion, 20-1
Griffin, Merv, 21
Griffin, Sandra, 171
Griffith, Andy, 226
Griffith, D. W., 196
Griffith, Melanie, 111, 128
Griffith Park, 192, 193, 196
Grifters, The, 174
Grodin, Charles, 217

Guilty by Suspicion, 20, 123, 203, 205
Gulls Way, 85

Hackett, Buddy, 56, 57, 107
Hall, Arsenio, 184
Hamilton, Linda, 93, 217, 236
Hanks, Tom, 174, 246
"Happy Days," 171
"Hardcastle and McCormick," 85
Harley Davidson & The Marlboro Man, 111
Harper, Valerie, 42, 63, 210
Harrelson, Woody, 42, 86
Harrison, George, 39, 40, 130
"Hart to Hart," 72, 215
Harvard/Westlake School, 41
Hasselhoff, David, 102
Hawn, Goldie, 89, 207, 212
Hearst, William Randolph, 101, 205
Heat, 100, 199, 200
Hefner, Hugh, 54, 89, 109
Hepburn, Katherine, 29
Herald-Examiner Building, 205
Heston, Charlton, 89
High Anxiety, 218
High Tower, 143, 144
Highland Gardens, 144
Hillside Cemetery, 106
Hilton, Barron, 40
Hitchcock, Alfred, 54, 61, 218
Hodges Castle, 85
Hoffman, Dustin, 122, 245
"Hogan Family, The" 211
Holden, William, 119, 155, 205
Hollywood and Vine, 155
Hollywood Bowl, 143

Hollywood Center Studios, 163
Hollywood Chamber of Commerce, 142, 147, 149
Hollywood Entertainment Museum, 147
Hollywood Heritage, 142
Hollywood High School, 152, 153
Hollywood Memorial Park Cemetery, 159, 161
Hollywood Reservoir, 189
Hollywood Roosevelt Hotel, 151
Hollywood Sign, 189
Hollywood Studio Museum, 142, 156, 165
Hollywood Walk of Fame, 147, 149, 155
Holy Cross Cemetery, 106
Hope, Bob, 226
Hopper, Dennis, 151, 244
Hotel Bel-Air, 45, 46, 47, 48
Houdini Estate, 182
"Doogie Howser, M.D.," 76
Hudson, Rock, 26
Hughes, Howard, 22, 43, 105, 123, 172, 242
Huntington Library, 215
Hutton, Barbara, 75, 102
Hyatt on Sunset, 125

In the Line of Fire, 199, 202
Indecent Proposal, 20, 86, 215
Independence Day, 199, 200, 202
Internal Affairs, 99
Intolerance, 196
Invasion of the Body Snatchers, 191
"It's a Living," 200

It's a Wonderful Life, 113

Jackson, Janet, 82, 146
Jackson, Michael, 98, 115, 146, 163, 206, 234
Jacobson, Laurie, 122, 145
Jagger, Mick, 41, 122, 173
"Jake and the Fatman," 86
James, Rick, 181
Jan and Dean, 107
Jazz Singer, The, 106, 159
Jenny, Ron, 93
John, Elton, 29, 63
Johnie's, 167, 168
Johnson, Kari, 142
Johnson, Magic, 98, 179
Jolson, Al, 106, 146, 234
Jones, Carolyn, 24
Jones, Tom, 45
Joplin, Janis, 10, 134, 144

Kaplan, Sam Hall, 203
Karate Kid III, 195
Kasssorla, Irene and Friedman, Norman, 55
Katzenberg, Jeffrey, 27, 82
Kaye, Danny, 29, 136
KCBS, 158
KCET, 160, 196
Keaton, Buster, 172, 221
Keaton, Diane, 122, 214
Keaton, Michael, 111, 146, 235
Keith, Brian, 83, 85
Kelly, Gene, 62
Kennedy, John F., 22, 69, 100, 101, 133, 171, 201, 208
Kennedy, Robert F., 22, 69, 174, 201
Keystone Cops, 173
Khashoggi, Adnan, 28

Kilmer, Val, 122, 200
Kindergarten Cop, 245
King Kong, 105, 191, 207
King, Rodney, 235
"Knight Riders," 215
"Knot's Landing," 236
KTLA, 159

"L.A. Law," 200
L.A. Story, 168, 174, 196
La Brea Tar Pits, 168, 245
Lakeview Medical Center, 236
Lady of the Lake, 174
Lamparski, Richard, 172
Landis, John, 26
Lasky, Jesse, 142
Last Action Hero, 244
Last Boy Scout, The, 208
Lautner, John, 183, 184, 185
Lawford, Pat, 100
Lawford, Peter, 100-1, 110, 130-1, 136
Leamer, Lawrence, 82, 87
"Leave It to Beaver," 229
Leaving Las Vegas, 192
Le Dome, 128
Led Zeppelin, 125
Lemmon, Jack, 30, 89
Leno, Jay, 30, 90, 137
LeRoy, Mervyn, 42
Less Than Zero, 175
Lethal Weapon, 134
Lethal Weapon II, 111, 183, 184, 200, 225
Lewis, Jerry, 45
Liberace, 124, 221
Life Stinks, 201
Linkletter, Art, 43, 128
Linkletter, Diane, 128
Little Brown Church in the Valley, 231

Little, Rich, 85
Little Richard, 125
Lloyd, Christopher, 211, 242
Lloyd, Harold, 30
Lockwood, Charles, 25, 28, 55, 188
"Lone Ranger, The," 191
Long Goodbye, The, 143
Los Angeles County Courthouse, 198
Los Angeles County Museum of Art, 168
Los Angeles Memorial Coliseum, 208
Los Angeles Sports Arena, 208
Los Angeles State and County Arboretum, 219
Los Angeles Valley College, 231
Los Angeles Zoo, 193
Lost World, The, 211
"Lou Grant," 202, 230
Lugosi, Bela, 106, 122

MacArthur Park, 175
"MacGyver," 173
Madonna, 18, 61, 87, 89, 98, 130, 155, 188, 190
Magic Castle, 144
Malibu Colony, 83, 84, 85
Malibu Gold Coast, 85
Malkovich, John, 167, 199
Mamas and the Papas, The, 41, 43
Man Trouble, 145
Mandeville Canyon Road, 71
Mann's Chinese Theater, 146, 148, 152
Mansfield, Jayne, 55, 244
Manson, Charles, 30, 31, 32

"Marcus Welby, M.D.," 100
Marshall High School, John, 195
Marshall, Penny, 113, 134
Martin, Dean, 45, 109, 126
Martin, Steve, 41, 61, 168, 193, 196, 214
Martin, Quinn, 134
Marx Brothers, 78, 119, 215
Marx, Groucho, 19
Marx, Harpo, 146
"M*A*S*H," 239, 244
Mass, Alex, 82
Matilda, 211
Mayer, Irene, 25
Mayer, Louis B., 45, 100, 101
Mayfield Senior School, 210
McClintock, David, 58
McCoo, Marilyn, 109, 110
McEnroe, John, 82, 83
McMahon, Ed, 25, 181
Medved, Michael, 77
Melcher, Terry, 31, 32
Melrose Avenue, 162
"Melrose Place," 53, 163, 169, 195, 245
Memoirs of an Invisible Man, 245
Menendez Murders, 62
Mezzalunna Restaurant, 67
MGM Studios, 102, 105
Midler, Bette, 60, 137
Million Dollar Theater, 203
Mineo, Sal, 118, 133
Minnelli, Vincente, 56, 129
Miracle Mile, 167, 168
Mr. Wrong, 202
Mitchell, Joni, 119
Mitchelson, Michael, 123, 133
Mobsters, 210
Mondrian Hotel, 126

Monroe, Marilyn, 22, 24, 56, 66, 69, 70, 109, 122, 123, 129, 133, 135, 174, 233

Montecito Apartments, 154

"Moonlighting," 111

Moore, Charles, 46

Moore, Demi, 82, 86, 179

Moore, Dudley, 61

"Mary Tyler Moore Show," 230

Moore, Roger, 123

Moorhead, Agnes, 37

Morgan, Julia, 205

Morrison, Jim, 107, 122, 125, 134

Morton, Charles, 215

Morton, Joe, 215

Morton's, 136

Mr. Baseball, 109, 208

"Mr. Novak," 195

Mr. Saturday Night, 174

MRX Pharmacy, 173

Mulholland Estates, 179

Mulholland House, 183

Murder in the First, 202

"Murder One," 111

Murphy, Eddie, 36, 57, 201, 214, 215

Music Box, The, 242

Musso and Frank Grill, 154

Mutual Benefit Life, 168

Naked Gun, The, 175

Naked Gun 2 ½, The, 66

Naked Gun 33 1/3, The, 207

National Enquirer, 110

National Lampoon's Vacation, 240

NBC Studios, 223, 224

Nelson, Ozzie, 145, 221

Nelson, Rick, 145, 184

Nelson, Tracy, 41

Newhart, Bob, 45

"Newhart Show, The Bob," 230

Newsies, 211

Nicholson, Jack, 136, 145, 179, 180, 181, 202

Nick of Time, 199

Nielsen, Leslie, 201

Nightmare on Elm Street, 240

9 to 5, 48

Niven, David, 76, 119

Nixon, 20, 175

Nixon, Richard M., 27, 69, 114

North, Jay, 213

Northridge earthquake, 235

Northridge Mall, 99

"Nurses," 245

Nutty Professor, The, 109, 201, 215

Occidental College, 218

O'Connor, Carroll, 89

Olmos, Edward James, 240

O'Rourke, Heather, 109

Other People's *Money,* 172

Ovitz, Michael, 89, 109

Owlwood, 55

Pacific Design Center, 136

Pacific Heights, 111

Pacific Palisades High School, 77

Pantages Theater, 156

Paradise Cove, 86, 102

Paramount Ranch, 239

Paramount Studios, 142, 147, 155, 161, 162

Parker Center, 205

Parker, Dorothy, 135

Parker, Fess, 120
Parker, Sarah Jessica, 122
"Partridge Family, The," 225
Pasadena City Hall, 212
Pasadena Public Library, 211
Pashdag, John, 33, 48
Patrick's Roadhouse, 102
Peck, Gregory, 40
Peninsula Beverly Hills Hotel, 114
Penn, Sean, 87
People vs. Larry Flynt, The, 42
Pepperdine University, 85
Perfect, 135
Perrenchio, Jerrold, 43
Perry, Luke, 66
Phillips, John, 41, 43
Phillips, Michelle, 43
Phoenix, River, 128
Piazza del Sol, 126
"Picket Fences," 242
Pickfair, 28
Pickford-Fairbanks Studios, 134
Pinkett, Jada, 199
Planet of the Apes, 89, 239
Playboy Mansion, 54, 55
Playboy Studio West, 127
Player, The, 123, 168, 217
Plunkett, Hugh, 20
Polanski, Roman, 32, 102, 122, 179, 181
Point Dume, 86, 91
Poitier, Sidney, 24, 25
Poseidon Adventure, The, 200, 244
Postcards From The Edge, 85, 236
Powell, Dick, 72, 134
Presley, Elvis, 19, 39, 49, 96

Presley, Priscilla, 19
Pretty in Pink, 201
Pretty Woman, 65, 123, 154
Prince, 19, 63
Prince, Hal, 63
"Pros and Cons," 123
Pryor, Richard, 145
Psycho, 229
Pulp Fiction, 243

Quaid, Dennis, 85, 244

Raft, George, 58, 172
Rainbow Grill, 129
Rainman, 200, 245
Raleigh Studios, 160
Randall, Tom, 221
Rasmusoon, Cecilia, 203
Ravenswood Apartments, 171
Reagan, Nancy, 42, 44, 75, 76, 120, 136, 231, 237
Reagan, Ronald, 42, 44, 75, 76, 111, 127, 129, 130, 136, 154, 160, 221, 231
Real Genius, 214
Rebel Without a Cause, 133, 173, 192, 195
Reeve, Christopher, 198
Reeves, George, 30, 33
Reeves, Keanu, 122, 202
Regent Beverly Wilshire Hotel, 65, 66
Reiner, Carl, 62
Reiner, Rob, 83, 109, 113, 134
"Remington Steele," 111, 230
Reservoir Dogs, 168
Return From Witch Mountain, 189
Reynolds, Burt, 39, 241
Reynolds, Debbie, 56, 223
Rialto Theater, 217

264

"Riptide," 243
Road to Singapore, The, 219
Roberts, Eric, 109
Roberts, Julia, 65, 154
Roberts, Pernell, 145
Robertson, Cliff, 58, 173
Robbins, Tim, 109, 123, 217
Rocketeer, The, 192
"Rockford Files, The," 49, 86, 203
Rocky, 173, 207, 208, 242
Rocky III, 201
Rocky V, 210
"Rocky and Bullwinkle," 120
Roddenberry, Gene, 46, 221
Rogers, Buddy, 28
Rogers, Mimi, 242
Rogers, Will, 24, 76, 77
Rogers State Beach, Will, 102
Rogers State Park, Will, 76
Rogers, Wayne, 24
Romy and Michele's High School Reunion, 174
Root, Eric, 60
Ross, Diana, 64, 146
Rowan, Dan, 39
Roxy, The, 129
Rubin, Jerry, 106, 115
Russo, Rene, 223
Ruthless People, 98, 136, 200
Ryan, Meg, 244

Santo Pietro, George, 178
Santo Pietro's Pizza, 178
Sarlot, Raymond, 120
Santa Monica Civic Auditorium, 98
Santa Monica Pier, 98, 99
Santa Monica Place, 99
Savalas, Telly, 39
Sayonara, 145

"Scarecrow and Mrs. King," 226
Scenes from a Mall, 137
Schatzi on Main, 97
Schenck, Joseph, 56
Schroder, Rick, 40
Schwab, Leon, 119
Schwab's, 118, 119, 153
Schwarzenegger, Arnold, 74, 76, 97, 98, 99, 146, 192, 199, 242, 244, 245
Scully, Vin, 75
Second Street Tunnel, 199
"Seinfeld," 174, 230
Selznick, David O., 25, 29, 75, 105
Sennett, Mack, 230
Serra Retreat, 83
"77 Sunset Strip," 126
Shatner, William, 77
Shepherd, Cybill, 111
Sherman Oaks Galleria, 233
Shoreham Towers, 128
Short Cuts, 168
Shrine Auditorium, 198, 204, 207
Shriver, Maria, 73, 76, 97
Shubert Theater, 110
Siegel, Bugsy, 58, 60, 123, 160, 188, 189
Silver, Joel, 195
"Silver Spoons," 38
Silver Streak, 205
Silverman, Jonathan, 113
Simpson, Don, 27, 46, 47
Simpson, O. J., 63, 67, 69, 71, 98, 199
Sinatra, Frank, 21, 39, 69, 89, 119, 133, 156
Sister Act, 143
Slotkin, Mark, 63

Smith, Jack, 153, 155
Smith, Roger, 126
Smith, Wil, 199
Sneakers, 210, 213
Snipes, Wesley, 151
Snow White and Seven Dwarfs, 196, 222
Someone to Watch Over Me, 244
Sonny and Cher, 41, 42, 55
Sony Entertainment, 105
Source, The, 122
Spada, James, 100, 110
Spago, 128
Species, 135, 201, 205
Speed, 202
Spelling, Aaron, 52, 53, 82, 169
Spelling, Tori, 41, 53
Spielberg, Steven, 75, 89, 238
Sports Connection, 135
Springsteen, Bruce, 29, 146
Squaw Man, The, 142
Stallone, Sylvester, 75, 89, 128, 173, 207, 210
Stand and Deliver, 241-2
Star 80, 109
"Star Trek," 147, 244
"Star Trek: The Next Generation," 98, 147
Star Trek IV, 77, 240
Star Trek VI, 191
Star Wares on Main, 96
Stargate, 244
Stenn, David, 61
Stewart, Jimmy, 39, 113
Stewart, Rod, 40, 61, 66, 128, 179
Sting, The, 98, 201, 229, 213
Stockwell, Dean, 202
Stone, Oliver, 107, 207

Stone, Sharon, 64
Streep, Meryl, 146
Streisand, Barbra, 40, 91
Sultan of Brunei, 22
Summers, Anthony, 101
Summit, The, 181
Sunset Boulevard, 119, 155, 162, 173

Tail o' the Pup, 136, 137
Tate, Sharon, 31, 32, 102, 106
Taylor, Derek, 130
Taylor, Elizabeth, 22, 43, 45, 61
Temple, Shirley, 41, 69
10 ("Ten"), 61
Terminator, The, 192, 198, 199, 216, 242
Terminator II, 93, 98, 99, 236
That Thing You Do!, 174, 246
"Third Rock From The Sun," 230
"thirtysomething," 217
Thomas, Bob, 124
Thomas, Danny, 19
Thomas, Marlo, 19
Thompson, Emma, 143
"Three's Company," 96, 193
Throw Momma From The Train, 231
Tiffany Theater, 126
Title Guarantee and Trust Building, 202
Todd, Thelma, 77, 78, 79
Top Hat Cafe, 153
Torrence, Bruce, 119
Tower Records, 128
Tracy, Spencer, 30
Travanti, Daniel J., 76
Travolta, John, 123, 135, 241, 243

Trebek, Alex, 183
Tri-Star Pictures, 105
Turner, Kathleen, 173
Turner, Lana, 60, 118, 119, 153
Turner, Tina, 146, 156
20th Century Fox, 111, 112, 113, 243

UCLA, 107, 109, 115
Unger Estate, 87, 88
Union Station, 205
Universal Studios, 229
University of Southern California (USC) 207

Valentino, Rudolph, 33, 61, 159, 160
Vallee, Rudy, 55, 184
Van Nuys High School, 233
Venice Beach, 96, 102
Vertigo, 201
Very Brady Sequel, A, 100
Villechaise, Herve, 219
Vinton, Bobby, 75
Volcano, 134, 168, 169

Walk in the Clouds, A, 212
Wallenchinski, David, 77
Walters, Barbara, 234
War of the Roses, The, 173, 214
War of the Worlds, 143, 203
Warner Bros., 134, 154, 155, 159, 224, 225
Warner Hollywood Studios, 134
Warner, Jack, 31, 36, 136
Wyman, Jane, 129, 221

Wasserman, Lou, 21
Wasson, Jake, 183
Wayne, John, 123, 234
Webb, Jack, 130, 221
Weintraub, Jerome, 86
Weismuller, Johnny, 41
Weltman, Manny, 182
West, Mae, 101, 171
Westin Bonaventure Hotel, 199, 200
Westward Beach, 89
Westwood Village Memorial Park and Mortuary, 109
Whisky, The, 129
What Really Happened to the Class of `65?, 77
White, Vanna, 178, 179
White Men Can't Jump, 96
Willat, Irvin C., 57
Willis, Bruce, 82, 111, 146, 179
Wild at Heart, 213
Wilson, Brian, 48, 81, 98, 244
Wilson, Dennis, 98
Wilson, Mara, 211
Wilson, Rita, 152
Wilson, Thomas, 217
Winningham, Mare, 168
Winters, Shelley, 133
Witch's House, 57, 59
Witches of Eastwick, The, 20, 214
Wolf, 202
Wolf's Lair, 189
"Wonder Years, The," 223, 231, 233
World According to Garp, The, 225
Zadora, Pia, 28, 179

PHOTO CREDITS

THE HOLLYWOOD BOOKSHELF

Books of related interest that can be ordered from North Ridge Books:

Hollywood Haunted: A Ghostly Tour of Filmland by Laurie Jacobson and Marc Wanamaker. A spine-tingling tour through the film capital's most memorable haunts. $16.95 (California residents add $1.40 sales tax.)

Hollywood Du Jour: Lost Recipes of Legendary Hollywood Haunts by Betty Goodwin. Profiles of and recipes from eighteen best remembered, but now closed, restaurants. $15.95 (California residents add $1.32 sales tax.)

Hollywood at Your Feet: The Story of the World-Famous Chinese Theater by Stacey Endres and Bob Cushman. With over 350 photographs. $19.95 (California residents add $1.65 sales tax).

Hollywood Goes On Location: A Guide to Famous Movie and TV Sites by Leon Smith. Walk in the footsteps of screen legends—Bogart's Casablanca, Nicholson's *Chinatown*, Swanson's *Sunset Boulevard*, Superman's Daily Planet—all in the Los Angeles area. $16.95 (California residents add $1.40 sales tax).

Following the Comedy Trail: A Guide to Laurel and Hardy and Our Gang Film Locations by Leon Smith. Includes exact addresses and maps. $16.95 (California residents add $1.40 sales tax).

Please send me the following books:

❏ Hollywood Haunted $16.95
❏ Hollywood Du Jour $15.95
❏ Hollywood at Your Feet: The Story
   of the World-Famous Chinese Theater $19.95
❏ Hollywood Goes On Location $16.95
❏ Following the Comedy Trail $16.95

Check the books you would like and add $3.00 shipping and handling for the first book; and an additional $1.00 for each additional book. The maximum shipping and handling cost is $7.50.

California residents must add 8.25% sales tax. Add $1.40 for Hollywood Haunted; $1.32 for Hollywood Du Jour; $1.65 for Hollywood at Your Feet; $1.40 for Hollywood Goes on Location; $1.40 for Following the Comedy Trail. (Please check your math very carefully. Incorrect amounts cannot be fulfilled.) Allow 4-6 weeks delivery.

Send check or money order payable to:
        NORTH RIDGE BOOKS
        P.O. Box 1463, El Toro, CA 92630

Cash or CODs will not be accepted.

Ship book to:

Mr./Mrs./Ms.   _____
Address   _____
City/State/Zip _____

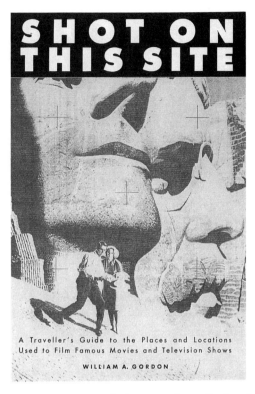

A Traveller's Guide to the Places and Locations
Used to Film Famous Movies and Television Shows

WILLIAM A. GORDON

SHOT ON THIS SITE helps tourists find where their favorite movies and television series were filmed. Covering over 900 sites throughout all 50 states, the book includes over 100 photographs, driving information, visiting hours (where appropriate), and insightful sidebars.

SHOT ON THIS SITE is available at most major bookstores. Or send $14.95 plus $3.00 shipping and handling to North Ridge Books, P. O. Box 1463, El Toro, CA 92630. CA residents add $1.23 sales tax.

Additional copies of

THE ULTIMATE
HOLLYWOOD
TOUR BOOK

can also be ordered by sending $15.95 and
$3.50 shipping and handling to:

NORTH RIDGE BOOKS
P.O. BOX 1463
EL TORO, CA 92630

California residents add $1.32 sales tax.

For overseas orders, please add $10.00
for air mail shipping and handling.